Near You

Robert N. Skond

**Also by
Robert W. Ikard**

No More Social Lynchings (1997)

Francis Craig
Dean of Southern Maestros

Robert W. Ikard

Hillsboro Press
Franklin, Tennessee

TENNESSEE HERITAGE LIBRARY
Bicentennial Collection

Printed in the United States of America

03   02   01   00   99   1   2   3   4   5

Library of Congress Catalog Card Number: 99-66051

ISBN: 1-57736-161-X

Cover design: Gary Bozeman

Unless otherwise acknowledged in the captions, illustrations are from the Francis Craig Papers, Special Collections Section, Jean and Alexander Heard Library, Vanderbilt University, Nashville, Tennessee.

HILLSBORO PRESS
an imprint of
PROVIDENCE HOUSE PUBLISHERS
238 Seaboard Lane • Franklin, Tennessee 37067
800-321-5692
www.providencehouse.com

To
Kitty

with gratitude for the
honor and pleasure
of living

Near You

contents

prelude

An Introductory Movement

In a family that strongly believed in genetics, I early concluded that my pleasure from and modest talent for music came from my mother. She was a childhood whiz on the piano and taught herself to play the organ at the Spring Hill, Tennessee, Presbyterian Church. In addition to her love for people and zest for repartee, this ability to tickle the ivories in whatever key you wished made her an inevitable life-of-the-party.

Her graduate recital at the Tennessee College for Women included works by Grieg, Beethoven, Chopin, Jadassohn, MacDowell, Glinka-Balakeriv, LaForge, and Liszt. Though I eventually could play a mean "Chicken Reel," it was obvious that her musical gift had not been passed whole to her eldest offspring. Perhaps my father diluted the genes, for, regardless his other attributes, he was tone deaf. Despite his good company, sitting beside him in church as he committed sacrilege on hymns was painful to a critical adolescent.

I loved music though and instinctively chose it as my favorite art form. In addition to Momma's piano lessons, there were various other musical stimuli intrinsic to our middle-class, small-town, southern milieu. Of course there was singing every Sunday. As my boyish tenor voice evolved to a limited range, pubertal bass, the repertoire segued from "Jesus Loves Me" to

"Onward Christian Soldiers" to "O God, Our Help in Ages Past," all in four-part harmony and conscientiously loud enough to drown out Daddy.[1]

I most enjoyed classical music heard on the old upright Zenith and recognized the necessity and pleasure of repetitive, analytical listening. Though perhaps unable to express the feeling, any child who will sit still long enough and has an intelligence slightly superior to an eggplant's will admire the mathematical counterpoint of Bach's *Art of Fugue*, the passion of Beethoven's *Ode to Joy*, or the pathos of Puccini's *Madame Butterfly*.

For too long I disdained the "country" (hillbilly, C&W, whatever) music which emanated from Nashville and surrounded me during my Middle Tennessee youth. Only after college did I come to value the interesting roots of the songs, deriving from my own Ulster-Irish heritage, or the occasional native genius of the musicians. Compare, for instance, Hank Williams's lyrics to Cole Porter's or Hank's ability to communicate with an audience to Henrico Caruso's. Why did I not recognize as I dressed every morning to radio tunes of Lester Flatt, Earl Scruggs, and the Foggy Mountain Boys that the organized chaos of bluegrass music was analogous to the Dixieland I later enjoyed in high school? Perhaps being too obsessed with the ostensibly prosaic lyrics pitched by their nasal voices, I also failed to discern that these boys had super virtuosity. The walls of conventional snobbery are hard to breach.

Then, though, there was band. The Columbia, Tennessee, public schools were blessed with a terrific band teacher, Mr. Tom Hewgley. In addition to teaching technical skills and musicianship, this personable, aggressive fellow maintained strict order and taught self-discipline. He was the boss; and, despite a modicum of talent, I seldom seemed on his good side. Still, I adored the martial and concert music we made and the perquisites of being in a crackerjack unit—travel, friendships, and community prestige. (The athletic teams might vary in quality over the years, but the Marching Lions were always the best.)

Mr. Hewgley was also a reputed dance bandleader in Middle Tennessee, heading several groups of good regional musicians.[2] After quitting that tiring weekend circuit, he bequeathed to his students some snazzy gray and red music stands and a thick library of stock arrangements. These were mostly "standards" of the 1930s and 1940s, with an occasional Dixieland number. With Mr. Hewgley's tutelage and occasional parental chaperonage, the CHS dance band in the 1950s played gigs in American Legion halls, armories, community centers, and the occasional country club in our and adjacent counties. No one pursued music as a career, though a tenor saxophonist later played some backup for the Everly Brothers. We were on our own; and, over several years of activity, there were no scandals or auto accidents. Bandsmen were just too scared of Tom Hewgley and their parents to misbehave.

As a senior, I was first trumpet and leader of this crew, bearing the responsibilities of making the saxophonists get along, staying awake during the early morning returns home, distributing the meager money earned, and urging the drummer to learn some Latin rhythm besides a beguine. In addition to the pleasure of playing, I also learned just how much joy there was in relating to a crush of sweaty dancers. As the hours and inhibitions passed, their smiles were broader, their clutches more intimate, their musical discernment less critical. Modulating their mood from an introductory "Sophisticated Lady" through "String of Pearls" to "In the Mood" or a raucous "Saints Go Marching In" and then descending through some ballads, "My Blue Heaven" or "Sentimental Journey," to a closing "Goodnight Sweetheart" felt just fine. It was sweet fun.

Nashville in the mid-1950s was "Music City, USA" for one reason—country music, coming mostly from WSM, the powerful, clear channel "Air Castle of the South," 650-AM on your radio dial. The Saturday night *Grand Ole Opry* attracted listeners with a nighttime signal that extended east to the Bahamas and west to the Rockies.[3] These increasingly popular broadcasts cemented the area's artistic reputation and attracted the performers, writers, and publishers who would create a major music industry in Nashville. The occasional reminder by those with broader perspectives that Nashville also had a symphony and a fine music school at George Peabody College was snuffed by the huge reputations of Roy Acuff, Eddy Arnold, Ernest Tubb, et al. National, if not regional, consensus was that this was a musically hick town. Important jazz or "pop" musicians gravitated to the big metropolitan centers, mainly New York and Los Angeles. There were no obvious local stars for youngsters interested in dance or "big band" music to emulate. These aficionados' late night listening had to come from careful dialing of distant stations in Cincinnati (WLW) or New Orleans (WWL), not WSM.

That powerful station then maintained a studio orchestra, and fans of music other than country recognized there was a nonclassical musical presence in Nashville other than the Opry. In addition to Beasley Smith, "Papa John" Gordy, and Owen Bradley, one occasionally heard of Francis Craig. He was inactive by the 1950s, but I was repeatedly reminded of him. My mother recalled his father had served in her hometown of Spring Hill during his peripatetic career as a Methodist minister. I knew he had written "Dynamite," the fight song of my school, Vanderbilt University. Then there was the indiscriminate use by disc jockeys of the appellation "immortal," as in Hoagy Carmichael's "immortal" "Stardust." Only in our neck of the woods, it was Francis Craig's "immortal" "Near You." I had no grasp of immortality, and the song was not in a league with "Stardust," but it did pop up on the airways quite a bit, long after its heyday. Though catchy and easy to sing, was it really immortal? Besides, who was Francis Craig?

I continued to hear of Craig during my adult life in Nashville. Perhaps it was the prevalence of that name in twentieth-century Nashville history. Among the principal founders of the National Life Insurance Company, which played an important part in making the city a financial center, were Messrs. C. A. and E. B. Craig.[4] Various founders' descendents had continued to lead the company until it was purchased by American General Insurance Company in 1982. Was Francis part of *that* Craig family, perhaps a blessed scion?

Though the Grand Ole Opry had been the broadcast signature since the late 1920s for WSM and National Life Insurance Company, there had been noncountry, live music broadcasts for most of the powerful station's history. Did Francis Craig provide any of that? If so, did the Craig connections have anything to do with such radio work?

A recurring Nashville business story from the 1970s into the 1990s was the financial struggle of the downtown Hermitage Hotel, one of the last elegant and historic southern hostelries. Every time insolvency or the wrecking ball loomed over the hotel, newspaper stories arose about the long and pleasant work of Francis Craig as leader of the house orchestra. How long, how good, or how important was that association? What is the history of house orchestras? Where did they go? Did really good or important musicians work in them? I considered these unknowns every time I enjoyed a sumptuous meal served by white-jacketed waiters in the Grill Room, the downstairs Hermitage restaurant where Francis Craig had provided a musical *digestivo* for generations of diners.

Through a "classic, big-band" format maintained in Nashville by station WAMB, listeners not only occasionally heard about Francis Craig but also numerous, famous alumni of his orchestra—Dinah Shore, Snooky Lanson, James Melton. Were there others? How important to their careers was their time with the Craig orchestra?

Many of those I interviewed for this work were incredulous that I believed writing about Francis Craig was worthwhile. Even without research, it was clear he could never be classified among the top national band leaders or composers. Duke Ellington or Johnny Mercer he was not. Some even wondered why I had not tackled a depiction of some regional musician whom the consensus had judged unequivocally "important." The answer lies in a stubborn, personal bias. I believe that importance, if not fame, can be found in the lives and careers of the most humble of us. Though perhaps paling when compared to Ellington, Mercer, and their ilk, even preliminary investigation revealed that Francis Craig's career was far from ordinary. For decades he had been "the man" who brought smiles and pleasure to those Middle Tennesseans whose toes tapped to popular music, and he had as well a certain national reputation. So the project was interesting to one who believed the beatitude that the meek would eventually get their cut (Matt. 5:5).

Francis Craig thus was a historical vacuum well worth filling by this amateur musician and fan of dance-band music whose trumpet chops had atrophied and whose facile feet had retreated from the dance floor. Said story should address at least the above noted facets, maybe others. Francis's life began at the dawn of the twentieth century and encompassed two world wars, the Depression, and the blossoming of the electronic entertainment industry, particularly radio. The majority of those working in the huge, contemporary Nashville music business are welcome emigrants to Music City but likely know nothing about Francis Craig. At his centennial in 2000, perhaps they should learn with me just what role this native son had in the launching of the music megalith of which they are a part.

Aside from his music and recordings, Francis Craig left a scant trail—not letters, articles, or diaries. Additionally, he was, despite a public life, very insular. It was, therefore, necessary to rely a great deal on the opinions of those who knew him. I have chosen to annotate interviews with less than academic thoroughness. Much of the information on Francis came from conversations with people from the same social stratum, mostly Nashvillians. Though I have listed all interviewees, I saw no value in identifying those with contrary opinions, when said compulsiveness might result in misunderstanding. It is the author's difficult task to seek the truth from narrative that invariably is at least somewhat subjective, and I gladly accept responsibility for any conclusions that might offend.

andante ma con brio

A Graceful Tempo, but with Spirit

Francis Jackson Craig was born in Dickson, Tennessee, on September 10, 1900, the ninth of ten children born to Robert James Craig, a Methodist minister, and Fannie Hewitt Frost Craig. After assuring the family that mother and newborn were doing fine, Reverend Craig was said to have offered a parlor prayer of gratitude and dedication: "Our Heavenly Father, we thank Thee for this new life delivered safely into our care and may he ever be dedicated to Thee and the service of his fellowman, Amen."[1] The one sentence petition was brief for the usually prolix pastor but well launched baby Francis down the straight and narrow path of whatever his life work would be. This was his world:

Aside from its being the eve of a new century, 1900 was in many ways a watershed year for the United States, a muscular, prosperous nation of over seventy-six million people. The youthful, western democracy brimmed with energy, hope, and optimism. The industrial revolution continued apace, and geopolitical events were pushing the U.S. to robe itself in an unaccustomed mantle of global responsibility and possible imperialism. The nation had won in 1898 the Spanish-American War. Victory had resulted in new commonwealth territories and established power credentials that would be soon codified by World War I. The world was rapidly shrinking as innovative marvels in transportation (trains, automobiles) and communication (telephones, moving pictures, phonographs) became generally available and affordable. The first overseas telephone call, from Key West, Florida, to Havana, Cuba, took place in 1900.

In addition to a calamitous fire in Galveston, regional newspapers on Francis's birth date depicted President William McKinley's acceptance in Chicago of the Republican nomination for a second term as president. He and his controversial vice-presidential nominee, Theodore Roosevelt, argued for maintenance of the gold monetary standard and promised a "full dinner pail" for all Americans. The opposition Democrat ticket of William Jennings Bryan and Adlai E. Stevenson again pleaded for acceptance of a free silver plank. As Francis arrived, the American Century was about to begin.[2]

There were over two million Tennesseans in 1900. By post-Civil War, southern standards, the state was relatively populous and prosperous. It boasted strong agricultural and manufacturing industries, which took advantage of central location and good transportation. In 1897, the state had (one year late) proudly celebrated its centennial with a huge six-month exposition in Nashville. Living up to its nickname of the Volunteer State, Tennessee had exceeded its enlistment quotas for the war against Spain. Though its people had split allegiance in the War between the States, Tennessee was more Dixie than Federal and was politically dominated by the Democrat Party. Tennesseans gave their electoral votes to Bryan a second time in 1900.[3]

Francis Craig's birthplace was representative of the Middle Tennessee villages and towns where Father Craig, as his descendents came to call him, spent his career and raised his children. Located some forty miles west of Nashville, Dickson owed its viability to U.S. Grant's insisting during the Civil War that a railroad be pushed from the Tennessee River to Nashville. That line went through Dickson, which, with a population of 1,363 in 1900, was the biggest town in its county. This populace was 84 percent white and nearly 100 percent Protestant. The county had a good hardwood timber industry, and its farmers produced corn, hay, small grain, tobacco, cotton, and fruits. Most living in town worked for the railroad or a firm that manufactured baseball bats and axe handles.

As there would be no automobiles in Dickson until after 1910, it did not matter a great deal that there were no paved streets. The town council authorized a local telephone system in 1899, and the first long distance call (to Waverly, twenty-four miles away) would take place in 1902. The council approved a brick sidewalk and a city water system the year Francis Craig was born. Locals paid one dollar per year to learn about all this in the weekly newspaper.[4]

At the propitious beginning of the century, Craig was to ride a wave of rapid, sometimes revolutionary development that ensued in many fields. As would be the case in technology, politics (beginning with the assassination of President McKinley and Theodore Roosevelt's assuming the presidency in September 1901), and business, music in the United States was poised in 1900 to evolve in directions quite different from anything known before. This was especially the case for nonclassical ("popular") music.

The most important influence on such music after the Civil War was the Negro. Not surprisingly, black musical expression during the last quarter of the nineteenth century derived from antebellum banjo music and spirituals. One of the groups that most successfully brought such music to the world's attention was the Fisk Jubilee Singers. When Nashville's Fisk University, established just after the War in 1866, was in financial straits, the student chorus performed a successful national tour in 1871 to raise the funds that kept the school afloat.

Though blacks participated for awhile in minstrelsy that had been established before the War, their new freedom and mobility led to unique forms of musical expression by century's end. Transposition of the pep and syncopation of banjo music and clog dancing to the piano resulted in "rags" or "ragtime" music. As with most new forms, it was initially derided as dangerous or decadent until its obvious charm overwhelmed the critics. Two of the most influential composers of ragtime music, Scott Joplin and Eubie Blake, published their best works, "Maple Leaf Rag" and "Charleston Rag" respectively, in 1899, one year before Francis Craig was born. In 1900, sheet music of "Maple Leaf Rag" was selling like hotcakes.[5]

Negroes found considerable opportunity for music making in the cultural potpourri of New Orleans. Black instrumental combos of five to seven pieces enjoyed plenty of work throughout the variegated racial spectrum. The "blues," another new contribution from black musicians, probably originated in New Orleans, springing from plantation spirituals. The music was technically even less structured than the somewhat loose organization of Negro hymns and succeeded in rhythmically portraying the uncertainty and pathos of its newly emancipated performers. Ma Rainey, one of its most seminal interpreters, claimed to have first done so before an audience in 1902, as Francis Craig was perhaps about to have his first haircut.[6]

Musically catalytic events were also taking place outside of the Southland in 1900. There was a huge market for lighthearted songs for theater, dance halls, and the ubiquitous parlor piano. Songs were now commodities. Victor Herbert was establishing a distinctive American musical theater. In New York City, the Witmark brothers led a migration of tunesmiths and publishers to West Twenty-eighth Street, soon to be known as Tin Pan Alley. Leading composers of the day were Paul Dresser, Charles K. Harris, and Harry Von Tilzer. At the same time there was such burgeoning productivity of new music, the struggle between writers and publishers for intellectual property rights was just getting underway.

Competition in sound technology was about to result in affordable music by the masters (e.g., Enrico Caruso and John Philip Sousa) in most parlors. The engineering and patent wars of Thomas A. Edison, Alexander G. Bell, and Emile Berliner over the last quarter of the nineteenth century resulted in a phonographic market that would grow over 700 percent during the decade beginning in 1900. Nearly a million cylinder and disc sound machines were produced in 1904 as the Columbia, Edison, and Victor companies vied for a seemingly limitless new market.[7]

Edison and others had also developed a method of rapidly projecting moving pictures during the late nineteenth century. Though not in Dickson, Tennessee, moving pictures were being seen in many cosmopolitan cities by 1900. The first picture show with a story line, *The Great Train Robbery,* was shown three years later. The new, popular medium would doom vaudeville, then the major outlet for popular music.[8] Few recognized that within a couple of decades movies would replace that market by many multiples.

A PREACHER'S SON

Francis Craig's parents were midsouthern Protestants. Robert Craig's family of Ulster-Irish heritage migrated to Middle Tennessee from South Carolina in the second decade of the nineteenth century. He was born in Giles County on October 3, 1854, the third of six children of William Jackson Craig and Virginia Borsor Abernathy. Other than the death of a sister, his childhood seems to have been idyllic. His devout Methodist father doubtless influenced his calling to the ministry.

Fannie Frost was born in Murfreesboro, Tennessee, July 28, 1862.[9] Her Frost lineage extended from England to New England in the early eighteenth century and thence to Middle Tennessee in the early nineteenth century. Her great-grandfather was an officer in the Continental Army.

Rev. and Mrs. Craig had outstanding educational credentials for their time. After attending Giles County public schools, Robert studied at Emory and Henry College in Virginia, where in 1875 he won the Robertson oratory medal. He then attended Vanderbilt University in Nashville. Both his universities were associated with the Methodist Church. During his one year (1875–76) in the Theological Department at Vanderbilt, he made some institutional history when he won the Founder's Day medal, also in oratory and the first presentation of the award. Founder's medals were eventually bestowed on those finishing first academically in the university's various schools.

R. J. Craig took pride in Vanderbilt, where four of his sons and one daughter later matriculated.[10]

Fannie Frost graduated from Soule College, a Methodist school which offered one to two years of advanced study and was the first institution of higher learning in Rutherford County.[11] She was considered musically gifted, developed some piano virtuosity, and worked as a music teacher. Her family rejected a proposed concert tour for her on advice from the family physician, who said her frail frame could never tolerate the rigors of travel. In 1880 at age eighteen, she married Robert Craig. Her bridegroom began pastoring a church in nearby McMinnville in 1879. Perhaps they met at some Methodist "social." Beginning in 1882, her allegedly frail constitution began healthily producing and raising their family of ten children. The Craigs obviously believed in being fruitful and multiplying (Gen. 1:28). Francis's eight older siblings were Bessie (1882), Carrie (1885), Virginia (1887), Robert Jr. (1890), Pearl (1893), William and Charles (twins, 1895), and Edward (1898). His baby sister was Catherine (1904).

Rev. Craig ascended into the Methodist Episcopal Church, South pulpit in 1876. Before his tenure in Dickson, he had ministered in Asbury, Port Royal, McMinnville, Bell Buckle, New Providence, Springfield, Waverly, Spring Hill, and Fayetteville, serving some fourteen churches in twenty years. These frequent moves were typical for clerics of his denomination and assured his children of a rural, southern, provincial youth. Though Rev. Craig's career was spent in such small town church stations (as Methodists designated them), he earned some ecclesiastical prestige and filled several leadership positions in church governance. Early on, he began serving stations rather than circuits, an assignment usually given the more gifted preachers and administrators. Later in his career, he was a presiding elder, a position akin to chief executive officer, at two different districts, Clarksville and Columbia. In addition to his administrative and ministerial activities, he occasionally contributed poetry to the church press.[12]

Thus, Francis Craig was born to intelligent, educated parents with broader intellectual and cultural perspectives than might be anticipated from their semirural heritages. Father and Mother Craig strove to nourish the intellects of their children with the best educations and opportunities available in Tennessee. This included attending private schools and instruction in music.

Young Francis seemingly had no interest or special aptitude for music until, at age eight, he shocked his mother with a display of spontaneous virtuosity. While walking by a pool hall in downtown Clarksville, Father Craig's current station, Francis heard the strains of a ragtime melody accompanied by the clicking percussion of colliding ivory orbs. He sauntered home and bowled over his mother by climbing onto the piano stool and playing what he had heard. After he twice repeated the performance, his sweet mother had to express some ambivalent incredulity. She was torn between amazement at his innate ability to translate tunes from his ear through his fingers onto the keys and her disappointment at his choice of music to play. Rag strains, not hymns or the classical music his older siblings had struggled with, had prompted this performance. She also recognized that Francis's father might not be necessarily charmed by the musical performance.

She was right. Rev. Craig took little solace in his child's amazing ability. He saw big evil in the rapidly evolving popular music, too readily available through player pianos and such iniquitous dens as pool halls. Concentrating instead on the lad's unique talent, the farsighted Mrs. Craig played the maternal ombudsman. She cleverly couched her opinion in biblical terms, reminding her husband that talents should be nurtured, not buried (Matt. 25: 15–29, Luke 19: 11–26).

She also instituted formal musical training for her son, hoping to direct his native ability into channels more appropriate for a preacher's boy. After the family's move to Pulaski when Francis was nine years old, she intensified the campaign against libidinous music. The church organ at which she labored sometimes lost its electricity and required manual pumping. She assigned Francis this standby duty, hoping such frequent exposure to sacred music would saturate his artistic soul by osmosis, crowding out profane popular strains.

The lad seemed to be advancing correctly on both technical and esthetic fronts. He was facile on keyboard drills and expertly played hymns and other nonfrivolous music. Parents Craig were smug about the apparently successful channeling of their talented son. Francis was especially proficient with his mother's favorite hymn, "Brighten the Corner." With considerable pride, Mrs. Craig arranged for him to play this acceptable piece for the ladies' Missionary Society, a very proper and appropriate audience.

The performance was both a shocking success and a parental embarrassment. Whether spontaneously or with uncharacteristic devious design, Francis politely played the hymn—in ragtime style! The ladies seemed to enjoy it, smiling, swaying, and unabashedly applauding. Mother Craig was crushed. All her efforts had been for naught. His artistic direction was instinctively set. Son Francis would be a musician, but he would do so in the manner he did and enjoyed best. Goodbye Isaac Watts; hello Scott Joplin.

Mrs. Craig apparently swallowed her disappointment and remained faithful to her earlier admonition to Mr. Craig that Francis's talent should be developed. Though his ability to play "by ear" was obvious, she recognized the need for instruction and found the best teacher for him in whatever town the parson's family alighted. If none was adequate or available, she carried on the lessons. His teacher in Pulaski was Cynthia Carter. In Gallatin, she was Prudence Simpson Dresser, a lady of considerable musical ability and breadth of vision. She stressed the necessity of piano drill and made him perform the classics in concert. Still, she did not object to the teenager's experimentation, first with rag, then blues. She wisely realized that her charge was not necessarily to change his direction but to make his playing as good as possible, no matter how he might apply it.[13]

Despite continued parental disapproval, Francis's fascination with popular music only increased through his teen years. In addition to an innate gift for musical pitch, rhythm seemed to ooze from the quiet but typically restless teenager. He would immediately retire to the keyboard after rushing home from school. Beneath a very composed façade lurked a normal, playful youngster. He taught himself to play the bones from the osseous remains of a supper beef roast. Francis's niece, Mary Elizabeth Lowe, daughter of his sister Bessie, was only seven years his junior. In addition to his pleasant nature and generosity, she remembered his playing hymns in ragtime fashion and being chided for such sacrilege by his mother. The PK (preacher's kid) was typically incorrigible.[14]

Craig *fils* supposedly achieved newspaper notoriety for the first time because of a potentially fatal accident involving the bold, new music of the jazz age. Sometime during the Gallatin tenure in 1913–1914, Father Craig had forbidden Francis to attend a jazz concert at the Masonic Hall featuring "Emory's Saxophone Orchestra, Memphis, Tennessee." This was a Negro jazz band! Despite his grudgingly increasing tolerance of Francis's frivolous musical tastes, such an event was much further afield than the staid minister could accept. For many months, somnambulism had been a problem for Francis. His parents had taken to tying his wrists to the bed. After falling asleep to the strains of the concert and in spite of the restraints, the frustrated young fan allegedly walked in his sleep toward the music and through an upper story window, falling to the yard onto his head.

Though alive, Francis was transiently unable to move his lower limbs. His doctor was aided in diagnosing the injury by a radiograph done with an X-ray machine transported to Gallatin from Vanderbilt Hospital, thirty miles away. Recovery was incomplete until some chiropractic manipulations. Francis resumed his normal, hectic life, playing football that autumn. He said that after the fall on his head, "I have been a musician ever since."[15]

Probably through 1913–14, Francis attended the Hawkins School in Gallatin, a boy's academy that placed emphasis on athletics and morals. The majority of his high school education was at the Massey School in Pulaski, his father's hometown. The twins had preceded him there. He boarded there and took a classic curriculum, including four years of Latin and two of Greek. Francis played various sports and was thought quite good at baseball. Massey teammates carried him off the field after a game won against Branham and Hughes after a timely hit by Craig. It did not hurt that the ball he struck got lost under some brush in the ungroomed outfield. He achieved his main extracurricular reputation, though, through his musical accomplishments. He graduated from Massey in May 1917.[16]

Francis was too young that summer to join the great patriotic World War I military enlistment stampede. His twin brothers, Charles and William, had left Vanderbilt to fight as Army officers in Europe. The disappointed youngest family male patriot had to be satisfied to serve briefly in the Student Army Training Corps (SATC) at Tennessee Polytechnic Institute in Cookeville, where his father pastored a church. Francis joined the army on October eighteenth, one month after his birthday. His enlistment document described him as being five feet seven and one-half inches tall (he had not achieved his full growth) and having a fair complexion, dark hair, and brown eyes. At discharge on December fourth, his character was called "excellent." The sixty dollars mustering-out money paid him by the army was doubtless helpful to the poor, imminent collegian.[17]

It is unclear how the educations of the Robert Craig children were financed purely by a minister's salary. The Craigs required all the children to do their parts. In addition to the home chores assigned all the brood, Francis worked at various jobs, including jerking sodas, and helped pay bills.[18] Perhaps Francis's father was given a ministerial discount at the various preparatory academies and colleges his children attended. As he diligently fulfilled his sacred obligations, Rev. Craig was said to have a cavalier attitude toward such mundane secular aggravations as debts, feeling that in the end God would provide. Some have suggested that his now wealthy siblings served as God's agents and aided the R. J. Craig family in various ways, including tuition payments.

THE (OTHER) CRAIG FAMILY BUSINESS

Aside from his immediate family, the primary influences on Francis Craig's career were in their historic infancies around the time of his birth. Perhaps the most important of these was one which could have assured him wealth and security if his father had not rejected the opportunity to participate in it. This was the National Life and Accident Insurance Company, a business that would become one of Nashville's most important forces and one with which Francis Craig's public inaccurately associated him throughout his life.

Two of Robert J. Craig's younger brothers, Cornelius Abernathy (C. A.) and Edward Burr (E. B.), were in 1901 among the seven purchasers of the National Sick and Accident Association, a company which specialized in industrial, or "Negro," insurance. Three of the seven, the two Craigs and Ridley Wills, had worked for the Tennessee Insurance Department. E. B. had been state treasurer and a deputy insurance commissioner in the 1890s. Wills had first worked as a clerk for E. B. and then become a deputy commissioner himself. It was Deputy Insurance Commissioner C. A. who informed the undercapitalized National Life in 1900 that it must reorganize from a fraternal into an assessment association. The company successfully transposed itself and seemed to be thriving, when its president died in 1901. His widow put majority stock in the company on the auction block.

From his perspective as a state regulator, C. A. knew the potential of this business, recognized an opportunity, and organized a syndicate to buy the company. Other alleged altruistic motives were his wishes to increase the insurance businesses located in Tennessee and to eliminate predatory practices of companies that had taken advantage by means of "industrial insurance" of poor, mainly black laborers since the Civil War. Depending on one's perspective, these policies were either prudent or predatory. There was no question they were profitable for their purveyors.[19]

Only a couple of the original investors had significant money. The Craigs did not. Before entering government work, C. A. had been a druggist. E. B. and Wills were out of government in 1901, employed by Virginia Iron, Coal and Coke Company. The best-heeled investor and the one who secured Nashville bank loans for several of the others was Mr. Newton White, a wealthy Giles County landowner and politician. The group placed a successful bid of $17,250 for the majority 115 shares on December 27, 1901, when Francis Craig was fifteen months old. The new board elected C. A. Craig its first president in January 1902.

Assets of the company, the name of which was changed later that year to National Life and Accident Insurance Company, were just under $23,000. By 1916, its assets were $2.3 million. Along with Life & Casualty, a similar company similarly founded by young men from upper South towns and villages, it would make Nashville a major insurance center. In addition to its business success, National Life would be noted for its abiding interest in and genuine contributions to its home city.

Rev. Craig's brothers supposedly offered him stock in National Life either at the time of purchase or through a subsequent stock offering early in the company's history. The ticket was one thousand dollars. R. J. apparently had no significant money and chose not to borrow any. He was notably disinterested in business, sometimes seeming to dreamily float above the practical realities most people sweated over. He apparently saw this pursuit of mammon as inappropriate to his clerical office. Equity investments in particular were deemed akin to gambling. The good reverend scrupulously resisted the temptation proffered by his capitalist brothers.[20]

Francis Craig was to realize big benefits from being a Craig, a family known for loyalty to kin. However, he did not experience the great wealth his cousins did from the insurance business. Though in later, insecure years he would be reminded ruefully of his father's altruistic choice, Francis Craig probably had no idea as a youngster that he had been assigned the economic high road.

ON TO UNIVERSITY

Francis Craig developed professionally rewarding, lifelong associations with several institutions. He clearly recognized their importance to him and demonstrated binding loyalty to National Life and its radio station, WSM, the Hermitage Hotel, and the university at which he matriculated, Vanderbilt.

Several of the Robert Craig progeny attended Vanderbilt. In addition to his father, Francis's sister Bessie and brothers Charles, William, and Edward preceded him at the school.[21]

Numerous cousins and succeeding generations of Craigs would also attend Vanderbilt, affirming the family belief, before the slogan was even coined, that Vandy was Dandy.

Father Craig had entered the Biblical Department in Vanderbilt University's first year of operation, 1875. For its first forty years, the university was under the auspices of the Methodist Episcopal Church, South. From Commodore Cornelius Vanderbilt's initial endowment of one million dollars in 1873 through contributions from the Carnegie and Rockefeller Foundations, the school owed its founding and early financial viability to northern philanthropy. This Yankee lucre did not promote any faculty or student body diversity. When Francis Craig came to Vanderbilt, its golden anniversary was approaching. During that era, most students had been middle to upper class Protestant males from the mid-South, mainly Tennessee. None had been Negro. Its faculty was mostly Methodist and philosophically "right of center."[22]

Vanderbilt was then moving in a new direction, guided by the visionary, though cautious chancellor, James H. Kirkland. This austere educator was the university's second chief executive, serving forty-four years, 1893–1937. Though a conservative, religious southerner, he had early recognized that Vanderbilt would never achieve the quality of the best universities unless he could enhance its finances and, more importantly, shed the shackles of religious dogmatism imposed by its Methodist-dominated board.

Vanderbilt had lost much of its initially nationally recognized academic luster during "The Ten Years' War" with the Methodist Church.[23] This struggle, beginning in the century's first decade, pitted a church that wanted strict philosophical control of the school, including curriculum and faculty, against the chancellor. Kirkland had no quarrel with Vanderbilt's Protestant tradition and constituency but recognized he would need a stronger, broader based board than envisioned by the church in order to escape the confines of Methodism. Though the church wanted to sponsor a university like those associated with older Protestant denominations, its relatively fundamental tenets were incompatible with the intellectual fervor characteristic of strong schools.

The bishops had also imposed an additional very pragmatic roadblock to academic improvement. They wanted total control through board selection by the Methodist General Conference without the nasty obligation of providing money. Kirkland recognized the limits of regional and church coffers and knew he could never appeal to northern foundations without providing a broader, secular academic program. The classical impasse between academic freedom and religious restriction was finally resolved in the Tennessee Supreme Court in 1914. After the court said the Methodist Conference did not have the authority to select Vanderbilt's board, the church narrowly voted to separate itself from the university.

Vanderbilt University had deteriorated during this struggle and was falling behind other prestigious southern schools in endowment, library volume, and faculty quality. All these problems were complicated by the disruption of World War I. However, Kirkland now had the atmosphere and latitude he needed and envisioned solution of all problems as Craig entered Vanderbilt. [24]

Vanderbilt was a cozy place. Some one thousand solidly southern students nestled into its Victorian Gothic buildings. Considering his family's history there, his familiarity with Nashville, and his excellent academic preparation, Francis was probably very comfortable at Vanderbilt. Father Craig had apparently saved enough to pay for his youngest son's freshman year but informed Francis that he would be responsible for paying his own way thereafter. Excluding food, books, clothing, and some possible deduction for his father being a minister, he would need to get his hands on approximately $400 for the fall term.[25]

When Francis entered Vanderbilt in the winter quarter of 1919, he had enough money to promptly pledge the Phi Delta Theta fraternity. Because his twin brothers had preceded him, he was a "legacy" of Tennessee Alpha, the first "Phi" chapter in the state. The Phis were also the first fraternity at Vanderbilt. They operated in secret as early as 1876, contrary to Vanderbilt policy. Officials gradually relaxed their proscription against fraternal organizations (as well as card playing and theater-going), and Vanderbilt Phi Delta Theta was officially chartered in 1883.

This traditionally strong fraternity attracted generations of young men, especially from the Nashville business and professional class, who became highly accomplished on the campus and in later life. Among Francis's frat brothers were two notable *literati*, Allen Tate and Jesse Wills. Both were members of the Fugitives, an important literary movement that arose from the Vanderbilt English Department. Wills also became president of National Life. Other brothers who became prominent in

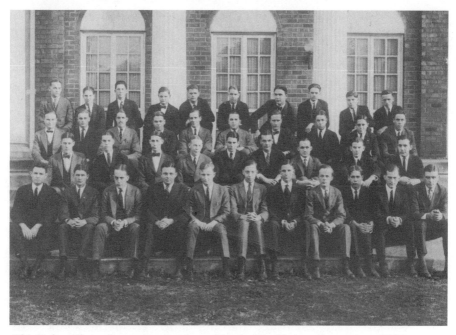

Phi Delta Theta fraternity members, Vanderbilt University, spring 1922. Left to Right—Front row: Robert Knight, Joe Clark, Bob McNeilly, Dan Dantzler, Tobe Woodruff, Jesse Wills, Elliott Adams, Allen Tate, James Waller, Tom Zerfoss, Hunter McDonald. Second Row: Charles (Slim) Embry, Bob Orr III, Bob Waller, Marvin Beard, Clarence Street, Charles Warterfield, Murphy Thomas, Brownlee Currey, Francis Craig. Third Row: Charles Woodruff, Edgar Sperry, Sidney Keeble, Charles Barham, Bill Leslie, Joe Landess, Walton Woodruff, Gorden Creveling, Frank Godchaux, Niles Coleman. Back row: Tom Griscom, Frank Fletcher, Saville Clark, Harris Sanders, Ed Webb, Ed Keeble, Joe Shapapd, Dan Street, Harold Knight, Emery Brockman. (Courtesy of Elizabeth Lancaster)

Nashville business circles were Ed Webb (National Life), Ed and Sidney Keeble (architecture and Life & Casualty Insurance respectively), Bob McNeilly (banking), and Brownlee Currey (Equitable Securities). If success in life truly is determined more by who rather than what you know, Francis had pledged an elite and potentially beneficial club. Numerous Craig cousins and in-laws would do the same over subsequent decades. Francis was loyal to Phi Delta Theta, and the national fraternity proudly recognized him throughout his career.[26]

Francis left Vanderbilt after the spring 1919 quarter. It may be true that, as Bowen Ingram asserted, this was necessitated by ill health (typhoid fever) and lack of funds. One tale that later circulated among his college peers was that he was so poor he could not afford to wash his bedsheets. By a term's end, the linens were rancid in odor and saffron in hue. Regardless of his supposed problems, however, he had no choice but to with-draw, for the university had requested it. Young Craig had demonstrated profound disinterest in higher academic accomplishment. His grades were abysmal. In his first two quarters, Francis's *highest* grades were Ds. Other than one-third hour for Reserve Officer Training Corps, he did not earn a single credit.

He recovered both health and solvency with the help of his brother, Captain Charles Craig. Charley garnered him a job working in the corral at Camp Grant in Rockford, Illinois. The army paid a munificent salary of $175 per month, and the vigorous outdoor work soon restored Francis's weight and strength. The shy, southern preacher's son also picked up some worldly ways, including gaming skills. From the soldiers he learned how to roll dice, becoming quite good at the "galloping dominoes." He returned to school more flush than his salary would have provided, apparently having profited from a lucra-tive aspect of the dreaded wages of sin (Rom. 6:23).[27]

Francis had not, however, reoriented himself academically. His 1920–1921 classroom performance was just good enough to allow him to stay in school. He did use his new skill at shooting craps to win his first car from a fraternity brother, Frank Godchaux. (Surely Father Craig did not learn of this!) It is unclear just what else he was doing with his time. He was not active on campus. Aside from his listing in Phi Delta Theta, the only mention of Francis Craig in any Vanderbilt publication was as a member of the Glee Club his freshman year. Neither was he a wastrel. No one ever asserted that even his collegiate behavior was anything other than temperate.

In place of studying, perhaps he was venturing out into the Nashville music world. Money remained a problem. Probably sometime in 1921 (various dates are recorded), he decided to use his musical skills, which heretofore had provided only pleasure for him and his circle, to pay the piper. He organized a band of three fellow students and five local professionals. The group's first job was a Sigma Nu fraternity dance, for which they were paid forty-five dollars. Though he may not have perceived it, Francis's career die was being cast.[28]

The band became active enough that it attracted the attention of the ever straight-laced Chancellor Kirkland. It is unknown what he thought about their music; his objection was to the band's name. Craig was probably not youthfully rebelling for the sake thereof when he called it the Vanderbilt Jazz Band. Kirkland apparently resented the presumptuous co-optation of the university's name, and he clearly did not appreciate its association with the word "jazz." For less than a decade, that term had been applied to the syncopated, improvisational music which followed ragtime in popular music chronology and had traveled from New Orleans to its 1920s epicenter, Chicago. The term, as well as the music, was in a state of evolution. It was also called *jass, jas, jaz,* and *jasz.* Its earlier roots evolved from slave jargon and had sexual connotations. Just as much as bootleg hootch, rising skirts, and rumble seat smooching, jazz represented 1920s licentiousness. Voices from the pulpit and podium railed against this quasi musical threat to public decorum and private virtue. This *was* the Jazz Age.

Kirkland probably did not invoke all these semantic and social subtleties in his reasoning about the controversy and surely did not recognize just how conservative and conventional Francis Craig was. Something about the situation struck a nerve though, and he concluded that neither Vanderbilt nor its Methodist heritage was about jazz.[29]

Kirkland allegedly upbraided the student maestro to change his orchestra's name or leave Vanderbilt. The chancellor's ultimatum, despite what many have written, probably did not precipitate Francis's pursuing a career as a musician. This was about the time Francis had decided he enjoyed being a bandleader and just might attempt making a living at it. His father had tremendous misgivings. He felt Francis would be the family black sheep for pursuing such a career. Most family members took this paternal opinion as a jest. Father Craig was not joking.

Francis claimed in a radio interview that the press of meeting eight o'clock classes and "three labs every afternoon" plus satisfying his booming dance band business was just too much, and one obligation had to go; so he quit school. That may have been, but Francis at that time really had no academic inclination whatsoever. In eight quarters of attendance at Vanderbilt, he earned fifteen and two-thirds credit hours. School was not his *schtick*. Perhaps Francis realized that a college degree was not a prerequisite for success as an orchestra leader. In 1923 a fellow named Glenn Miller was cutting short his college experience at the University of Colorado after blazing a trail of academic mediocrity[30]

Francis changed the band's name to Francis Craig and His Orchestra and left Vanderbilt's hallowed halls after the spring quarter of 1922. Despite Vanderbilt's numerous later proud allusions to his graduation, neither he nor any of his siblings earned a degree from the university. Bessie left after three years of study. The twins never returned after going to war. Edward accepted an appointment to the Naval Academy in 1918 after attending Vanderbilt two years.[31]

A LIFE'S WORK

Throughout his career, Francis Craig was firmly in control of his band. He made all artistic and business decisions. Though he doubtless sought advice, he kept his counsel and ran a taut, reliable orchestra. The compulsiveness, prudence, and energy with which the young man immediately managed his first professional group were the opposite of the way he had performed as a student. Francis seemed a natural orchestra leader, having an aptitude almost as innate as his ability to play piano by ear.

He certainly looked the part. Now grown to his full height of five feet ten and one-half inches, he was a handsome man with sharp, even features, dark eyes, and a slim physique. When garbed in a tuxedo and with his hair slicked down, Francis Craig could pass for an undergraduate swain at a fraternity party, a mysterious silent screen Lothario, *or* the leader of a society orchestra.

Until an unexpected professional bonanza late in his career, Francis supposedly never had an agent or advance man. He did it all himself or paid a trustworthy band member a bit more to help with business. The steady flow of engagements his band earned and played soon after its launching cannot, therefore, be attributed to shill or, at that time, strong friends in high places. They were just good at what they did, playing dance music pitched to a target audience of mostly well heeled southerners. The band was also reliable. Francis fulfilled his contracts and paid his players on time. How much he paid them became an endless topic of musician gossip. His penurious background makes understandable a personal characteristic for which he early became noted, parsimony. Perhaps this trait made him too cautious in business matters, but it would also help him sail past some financial shoals during dicey economic times. Francis Craig had many virtues; one was prudence (Prov. 14:15).

Even before Francis left school, the orchestra's reputation had gone beyond Vanderbilt's fraternity row. They had begun making regular appearances at Nashville's exclusive Belle Meade Country Club, another of the institutions with which Francis's business and name became rewardingly associated. The Belle Meade Club evolved from the Nashville Golf and Country Club, Nashville's first golf club, founded in 1901. After being induced to move out Harding Pike to the new Belle Meade subdivision in 1916, the club prospered and changed its name to Belle Meade Country Club in 1923, the year Craig set sail into

Francis Craig, handsome young orchestra leader. (Courtesy of W. Lane Abernathy)

his career. As would be the case throughout Francis's career, most of Nashville's business and professional elite, including C. A. and E. B. Craig at that time, were members at the Belle Meade Club.[32]

1923 was indeed a very good year for Francis Craig. The orchestra's reputation quickly grew throughout the mid-South, and they were soon busy playing debuts, college and fraternity parties, and country club dances in North Carolina, Georgia, and Alabama, as well as Tennessee. About the time he was scheduled to receive his diploma from Vanderbilt, he was instead enjoying steady, independent work at the Cascade Plunge Pool, a combination swimming, dinner, and dance club, in Birmingham, Alabama. He made that summer another, even more important life decision, the choice of a wife. By all accounts, he did real well.

Elizabeth Lazynka Gewin was the oldest of four daughters of Dr. and Mrs. William Christopher Gewin. Her father was a prominent Birmingham surgeon, who had founded the Birmingham Infirmary (later Baptist Hospital) and was one of the first in the South to use radium to treat malignancies. Dr. Gewin did well in real estate investments, and Elizabeth's family was significantly more prosperous than Francis's. Her family on both sides had a strong southern heritage. Both of Elizabeth's grandfathers fought for the South in the War between the States, one riding with Nathan Bedford Forrest at Brice's Crossroads.

In the summer of 1923, she was on vacation after her freshman year at Goucher College in Baltimore, Maryland. In 1998, Craig's widow was uncertain whether she met the young orchestra leader at the Cascade Plunge or the Tutwiler Hotel. Bowen Ingram described a cute scene in which Elizabeth complimented "Mr. Craig" on his wonderful music as she danced by in the arms of another. The maestro almost reflexly turned the baton over to a band member and broke in on the gorgeous coed's partner. Regardless of the site or circumstance, they were immediately and irretrievably smitten. Francis dated her that summer and pursued her throughout her sophomore year, sometimes visiting Baltimore when the band was on the East Coast.

Elizabeth Lazynka Gewin as a Goucher student. (From her scrapbook)

Neither had any doubts about the choice of the other. The Craig family certainly approved of the match. Father Craig urged Francis to treat his bride as a lovely flower and to prove himself worthy of the devotion of a good woman. Goucher's dean chided Elizabeth for leaving college after her second academic year to marry. She responded that she was in love and must do so, for she had met a "prize package." Presumably Francis saw in Elizabeth those characteristics for which she was reputed through her life. In addition to her obvious beauty, she was an elegant, intelligent, resourceful, strong, and cordial woman—the very model of a southern lady.

They were married in the Gewin home on the Monday evening of October 20, 1924. A private betrothal attended only by family and a few friends was held instead of a church ceremony because of the recent death of Elizabeth's maternal grandfather. Father Craig presided, and Charley stood as Francis's best man. After a reception, the newlyweds headed to New Orleans and other points south for their honeymoon.[33]

The couple began their married life in Birmingham. Considering his love for and his early success in music, Francis surprisingly succumbed to pressure from both his and Elizabeth's families to leave it. Through Gewin family connections, he got a sales job with the Columbus Marble Works. Francis had resisted this career change toward respectability and security. His concern was appropriate. He was ill fitted for and miserable in the work. Sometime in the first half of 1925, he persuaded Elizabeth to return to Nashville with him. Though recognizable employment did not await him there, he informed his bride that he would only be happy leading an orchestra.[34]

Francis and Elizabeth came to Nashville to seek but were uncertain whether they would find (Matt. 7:7). They had all the economic trepidations of any young, middle-class couple. Both were conservative and responsible. Francis was far from the caricature of most professional popular musicians. He did not drink, had a long-term perspective, craved security, and wanted to have a family with Elizabeth. They surely knew that the band business was unpredictable and that far more musicians ended up selling insurance or teaching music to distracted students than playing in Hollywood or New York. The Craigs were a tandem, though, and prepared to face life's uncertainties together.

Father Craig's remonstrations against a member of his reputable family pursuing the popular music business had not softened. According to him, there was no doubt that such a job was beneath the classical professions his children should pursue. In addition to the obvious financial insecurity of such work, he questioned the intrinsic value of jazz music, either to the purveyor or partaker. R. J. was certain his son was doomed to poverty and, worse, unfulfillment. He was not the only family member so concerned. For several years after his return to Nashville, Uncle C. A. inveigled him to come into the family's respectable and booming insurance business.

Francis could not imagine just how fortuitous the career reorientation would be. Perhaps he consulted a (then popular) Ouija board and saw that a return to the music business in Nashville would accentuate his positives and eliminate many of his negatives. Opportunity there was to be enhanced by a booming national economy, a public yen to dance, family connections, technological innovations, and a unique job that would provide security in good times and bad. Francis decided to bring his bride home to the Athens of the South, which in no small part due to his own work, would come to be better known as Music City USA.[35]

allegretto

A Light, Cheerful, Fast Tempo

When Francis Craig returned in 1925, the economy was fat and the society hot. It was not the worst of times to begin a career in Nashville, Tennessee, U.S.A.

The United States were midstride into the Roaring Twenties. After rejecting Woodrow Wilson's League of Nations, the U.S. turned inward to enjoy a booming economy and all its attendant social changes. Increasingly efficient manufacturing, epitomized by Henry Ford's assembly-line methods, and spreading availability of electric energy brought affordable creature comforts to a growing middle class. Among such products were telephones, phonographs, radios, and cameras (still and moving), that created a communications revolution—a fortuitous opportunity for entertainers, including Francis Craig.[1]

Americans used all these technical innovations to *play* and, in the process, transgress traditional social boundaries. Women's attire became loose, short, and revealing—symbolic of their increasing economic and behavioral emancipation. The availability of jazz via radio and phonograph led to a dancing craze. Affordable automobiles freed young people from the parlor's confines. Despite the misguided prohibition of alcohol by the Eighteenth Amendment to the Constitution at the advent of the decade, the public winked and consumed

24

more and more booze, usually to the benefit of criminal entrepreneurs.

Changes in popular music proceeded at the same *accelerando* pace. Once more, Francis Craig was serendipitously present "In the beginning . . . " (Gen. 1:1). As dancing became more popular, musicians struggled to understand just what a dance band should be. They began by replacing strings with wind instruments. Jazz bands in the twenties usually had five or six men. A cornet, saxophone, or clarinet player provided most of the melody. Piano, drums, banjo, and tuba supplied the rhythm and occasional riffs. Larger combinations of ten or more musicians played scored, rarely improvisational, "sweet" music. Such bands were more commercially successful, playing engagements in the better clubs and hotels.

The national center of jazz had moved from New Orleans to Chicago. Though most jazz players were black, the recordings of the Original Dixieland Jazz Band, a white group, initially stimulated broad public interest in the music. Key Chicago jazz groups in the first half of the decade included King Oliver's Creole Jazz Band with Louis Armstrong, the Wolverines with the brilliant but doomed Bix Beiderbecke, and the Austin High Gang with Jimmy McPartland, Eddie Condon, and Gene Krupa. Technology was stimulating change in the music business. Because of better broadcast and distribution facilities, the main action moved to New York in the latter 1920s.

Paul Whiteman was the ultimate "crossover" musician of the decade, profitably bridging the gap between sweet and jazz strains for the public. He did this with a stable of large orchestras, usually containing full string sections. The apogee of this effort was the "Experiment in Modern Music" concert at the Aeolian Hall in New York on February 12, 1924. Though the program began with "Livery Stable Blues" and ended with Edward Elgar's "Pomp and Circumstance," the musically revolutionary moment was the introduction of George Gershwin's "Rhapsody in Blue." Besides cementing Gershwin's national reputation, the piece was a seminal American effort at incorporating popular musical strains into so-called serious music. A century and one-half of American democratization and societal amalgamation had culminated in legitimization of a popular music form, the blues, taking it from New Orleans's wharves and Chicago's speakeasies to the respectable New York stage. It was now not only fun to swing; it was entirely correct.

Gershwin and his brother, Ira, barely stood out from a host of successful writers for the musical theater business, which thrived before the advent later in the decade of sound in movies. In addition to the Gershwins, the best songs of this frenetic decade were written by Irving Berlin, Jerome Kern, Cole Porter, Richard Rogers, and Larry Hart. Orchestras in clubs, records, and (later) radio disseminated their tunes to parlors and parties as a liberated, prosperous nation jumped, swayed, and sweated to subliminally sexy dances like the shimmy, Black Bottom, and Charleston.[2]

Largely because of the Scopes trial in 1925, Tennessee would be cast again as a backwoods haven for fundamentalist illiterates. However, the Volunteer State in the twenties was undergoing considerable socioeconomic change. Cynics from without who derogated the state overlooked an important contribution to national civil rights made by Tennessee's citizenry at the dawn of the decade. In summer 1920, the state legislature passed the Nineteenth Amendment to the U.S. Constitution. Tennessee was the thirty-sixth state to approve the amendment, thereby assuring its passage and national women's suffrage. Eight southern states has previously rejected the amendment. Both pro- and anti-suffragists had important headquarters in the Hermitage Hotel, an institution central to Francis Craig's career.

Bracketed between the immediate post-World War I inflation and the economic depression of the 1930s, the state participated with the nation in a decade of growth. In 1929, its three major cities produced manufactured goods worth $450 million. Tennessee population growth during the decade was only 12 percent, from approximately 2.4 million to 2.6 million. More important, the state became increasingly urban, fleeing the farm for the city. Those folks were going to need entertainment.[3]

World War I had been invigorating for Nashville. Its business class was wealthy but remained generally cautious, perhaps explaining the city's eclipse in regional power and population after the War between the States by Atlanta, Birmingham, and Memphis. Still, by 1920 the city had a population of almost 120,000 and would grow to 150,000 by 1930, a whopping 30 percent increase. Though its leaders did not build on the promising industrial base of the Old Hickory Munitions Project built by E. I. DuPont Nemours Company in the Great War, the city attracted numerous basic manufacturing industries such as clothing and shoes from the labor-expensive North.

The versatility of Nashville's economy was highlighted by its rapidly expanding service sector, including higher education, insurance, and banking. Numerous black and white colleges and universities, especially Francis Craig's Vanderbilt, made Nashville a stimulating place and provided recurring crops of civic-minded intelligentsia. Life & Casualty and National Life developed more reputable and expensive insurance policies commensurate with the public's increased purchasing power and cast their sales forces far beyond the upper South. Nashville's bankers shed their stodgy image during the 1920s, increasing their clearings 280 percent between 1915 and 1929 and causing boosters to call Union Street the "Wall Street of the South."

To Craig's benefit, Nashvillians had more money and, like the rest of the country, were ready to spend it on goods and entertainment. They even dabbled in installment buying, a new, sophisticated consumer practice formerly anathema to traditional, pay-as-you-go southerners. Department stores and cinemas blossomed downtown. By 1930, approximately 28 percent of Nashville families owned a radio. Of more economic import, people were purchasing more automobiles and taking motor trips, especially to the big cities such as Nashville. On returning to Nashville, Francis and Elizabeth bought their first car, a Ford Model T. Thanks to Henry Ford's assembly-line production techniques, that vehicle sold for around three hundred dollars.[4]

Absolutely no great musical waves were flowing from Nashville in the early twenties. Traditional folk music did not yet have a significant outlet beyond the region. Folks in the Bible Belt were as fun loving as others; but conservative, southern mores mostly kept a lid on things. New York City or Chicago the place was not! Surely in this simmering and familiar economic pot though, Craig could still enjoy making music and provide a living for his family. There seemed to be numerous venues in which he could realize his artistic and economic goals. Anything would beat selling marble.

THE HERMITAGE HOTEL

Only a few pages after freshman Francis Craig's listing in the 1919 Vanderbilt yearbook, the *Commodore*, was an advertisement for the Hermitage Hotel, "Nashville's New Million Dollar Hotel." The proximity of man and institution was to persist for three decades.

The hotel had opened in September 1910 to fanfare for its elegance and modernity. Located downtown only one block from the Tennessee Capitol grounds on the corner of Sixth Avenue and Union Street, it was ten stories tall, had 250 rooms, served only distilled water (to prevent typhoid fever), and was said to be noise proof and, because of its concrete floors, fireproof. There was a 250-seat convention hall on the top floor and writing desks on the mezzanine. A unique promenade and lounge area called the "Loggia" extended across the east front of the first floor. Boosters loved the hotel, calling it " . . . one of America's noted hostelries."

Architect J. E. R. Carpenter, a Columbia, Tennessee, native had designed the structure. He spent most of his professional career in New York but was responsible for many of the most recognizable and appreciated buildings in Middle Tennessee. These included the Maury County Courthouse and Columbia Military Academy in Columbia and St. Thomas Hospital, the Stahlman Building, and Vanderbilt's Kirkland Tower in Nashville. The influence of his study at the Ecole des Beaux

Arts in Paris on these structures and the Hermitage was obvious. The Hermitage was said to be the only commercial Beaux Arts building in Tennessee.

Through a terra cotta façade, a visitor entered arched openings between coupled columns into a foyer that led up a few stairs to a thirty-foot vaulted lobby, which featured a huge, stained glass skylight with surrounding glass panels, Tennessee marble floors, and Italian marble columns. The lime green and black glass finish on the floors and walls in the men's restroom were especially gorgeous. Other characteristics included extravagant French Renaissance detailing, egg and dart and dental moldings, cut velvet upholstery, and plasterwork with festoons, garlands, plaques, and the hotel monogram. Visitors could also descend from the foyer to a downstairs relaxation area. Dark Circassian walnut paneling and wainscoting gave a more informal flavor to the low-ceilinged Grill Room. Glowing through the subdued subterranean light were brass fixtures on the adjacent, similarly appointed gentleman's bar.

At the grand opening, manager Timothy Murphy had welcomed swells from Nashville and points beyond to an elegant banquet served on white linens with fine silverware. Guests were assured that all the help except kitchen staff were white and that locals were hired whenever possible. They especially seemed to appreciate dinner music by visiting musicians from New York's Waldorf-Astoria Hotel, a feature the management suggested might be maintained.[5]

HOTEL HERMITAGE

Nashville's New Million Dollar Hotel

Fireproof—Strictly Modern in Every Appointment

250 Rooms	250 Baths

EUROPEAN

Each apartment is complete and provided with every facility to meet the wants of our patrons. Centrally and conveniently located to both the wholesale and retail districts

**Beautiful Dining Room
Grill Room and Ball Room**

RATES: $2.00 AND UPWARD

| R. R. MEYER | R. E. HYDE |
| President | Manager |

Advertisement for the Hermitage Hotel from the Commodore, *1919.*

Though not on a regular basis, Francis Craig had played at the Hermitage Hotel during his brief prenuptial music career. This was usually in the ornate ballroom adjacent to the lobby. His first music job overture after his return home was to the hotel's management. It paid off in spades. He landed a position playing in the Grill Room for lunch and dinner. The orchestra would occasionally entertain for more formal occasions upstairs, but the Grill Room was to be Craig's office for most of the next couple of decades. He had a steady job—as a musician.

For a popular orchestra, a hotel job was in 1925 a real plum. Many of the dance bands that formed after World War I were known by the establishment where they regularly played. In addition to the Waldorf-Astoria Orchestra, led by Joseph Knecht, other popular groups were Erdody's Hotel Pennsylvania Orchestra, Abe Lyman's California Ambassador Hotel Orchestra, Vincent Lopez and His Pennsylvania Hotel Orchestra, and the Bar Harbor Society Orchestra. These bands were the commercial pacesetters of the era, and Francis was prudent to emulate them.[6]

Francis enjoyed the relaxed, convivial work of playing soft music for diners, a mood in tune with his increasingly sedate adult personality. He and Elizabeth were ecstatic. The engagement was the Craigs' first as a team and represented, then and later, pleasurable security. From the beginning, both developed loyalty to the Hermitage and its longtime manager, Howard Baughman—to the mutual benefit of employer and employee. A generation of Middle Tennesseans and (some very important) travelers would

The Hermitage Hotel. (From the Nashville Tennessean, May 6, 1979)

pleasurably associate Francis Craig and His Orchestra with the Hermitage Hotel.[7]

THE AIR CASTLE OF THE SOUTH

F rancis Craig hit the ground running in Nashville. In addition to his regular job at the Hermitage, he was quickly playing for country club (mainly Belle Meade) dances, debuts, and college and high school proms. Craig was in demand at numerous southeastern schools during the twenties, including the University of the South (called Sewanee or "Swawnee" by locals), Alabama, Tennessee, North Carolina, North Carolina State, Auburn, Georgia, and Georgia Tech. Conveniently, he did lots of college work at Vanderbilt, where he was very popular. He played for most of the fraternity dances. In 1929, his was the first local orchestra to play the Vanderbilt finals dance.[8]

There was even a several week engagement his first summer back in business at Willow Beach, a resort near Little Rock, Arkansas. For one of the few times in their marriage, Elizabeth accompanied Francis to this extended job. He covered his Hermitage obligations when out of town by using substitute musicians. Whenever he was in Nashville though, he was working in the Grill Room.

Whether for esthetic or economic reasons, the band's instrumentation straddled the gap between that of a small jazz group and the bigger, more sedate orchestras. Craig had eight players at his 1923 Birmingham Cascade Plunge engagement and nine when he played the Willow Beach at Little Rock in 1925. The latter orchestra had three brass, three reeds, piano, drums, and the popular 1920s instruments, tuba and banjo, on which somebody doubled. With this versatile coterie, Francis could provide sweet or swinging, but rarely truly hot, music.

On June eighteenth, the Craigs paid $9,500 for a clapboard, bungalow-style home built in 1923 on 3822 Whitland Avenue in the fashionable west end of town. They paid

Francis Craig's band at Willow Beach, Little Rock, Arkansas, 1925. Left to right: *first three unknown; Francis Craig, leader/piano; Powell Adams, drums; Percy Carson, banjo; James Melton, sax/vocal; Jack Hamilton, sousaphone. (From P. J. Broome and Clay Tucker,* The Other Music City, *1990)*

$2,230 in cash, assumed a mortgage for $4,500 and took out two $1,385 notes from the seller. Though not commodious, it was big enough to allow family boarders for years. Brother Robert stayed with them for several months. The retired Father Craig and Fannie stayed in the house while Francis and Elizabeth were in Little Rock and "just never left," until moving to Florida in the mid-1930s. Elizabeth enjoyed having her in-laws in the home, considering them good company as well as family.[9]

Francis Craig had a wife, home, automobile, and employment. Surely his cup could not runneth over more (Ps. 23:5). Oh, yes it could!

There was another seemingly visionary advertisement in Craig's last Vanderbilt yearbook. In the 1923 *Commodore*, National Life and Accident Insurance Co. presented a financial statement showing capital and surplus of $1.36 million. The Company was on the move. Francis may not have been one of the insurance Craigs, but he was about to hitch his wagon to that family star.

On September 11, 1899, almost exactly one year before Francis Craig was born, the Italian boy genius Guglielmo Marconi arrived in New York City to convince the United States military about the value of wireless, long-distance communication. This was an opportune time for such a campaign. Marconi's arrival was overshadowed by New York's preparations to welcome Admiral George Dewey, the hero of the Battle of Manila Bay during the just ended Spanish-American War. Land and sea communications had been distressingly inadequate during that conflict.

During the previous decade, Marconi had developed transmitters and receivers between which Morse code could be transmitted by "Hertzian" (later dubbed "radio") waves. He had received a British patent for his system in 1897 and had demonstrated the efficacy of it to the British Navy before he came to the United States. He would be the first to demonstrate the feasibility of intercontinental "telephony" by transmitting the letter "S" from Cornwall to Newfoundland in 1903. The age of radio had begun.[10]

Though corporate and government money and expertise were important, most early strides in radio technology were by a few gifted scientists who hungrily explored the mysteries of the new medium. Until heavy government regulation of radio traffic in the World War, development was unfettered and rapid. By 1906, Reginald Fessenden was able to transmit sound from Brant Rock, Massachusetts, to ships. Improvements in tube technology by the Marconi Company and Lee De Forest allowed Mr. De Forest to broadcast as far as five hundred miles from the Eiffel Tower in 1908. De Forest created even greater excitement with the broadcast in 1908 of

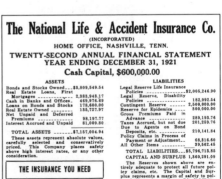

Advertisement in the Commodore, *1923.*

Enrico Caruso singing from the Metropolitan Opera House to clusters of listeners sharing earphones in New Jersey and New York City. The public was spellbound by the single link to the *Titanic* disaster in 1912 established by the twenty-one-year-old telegrapher David Sarnoff from his American Marconi station in New York's Wanamaker Store.

Radio clubs sprang up in Boy Scout troops, schools, and small towns in the hinterland. Entirely analogous to the ease which their descendents would master computers before their parents, youngsters inspired by Marconi's accomplishments and the glamour of "wireless" ensconced themselves in barns, attics, and sheds to explore the ether. These hobbyists would be prominent among the scientists, entrepreneurs, and executives who fueled the post-World War I boom in the radio business. Their work was temporarily stopped by the War, as the Government restricted channels, enlisting them for solely military communication.[11]

After the War, the Westinghouse Company recognized that there might be a general market for "wireless telephones," advertised in Pittsburgh as "Amateur Wireless Sets." In order to stimulate sales of these receivers, Westinghouse created a radio station in Pittsburgh, to which the Department of Commerce assigned the letters KDKA. They rushed its installation in order to broadcast the results of the 1920 election. In choosing Warren Harding over James Cox, the country seemed to be reaffirming its rejection of internationalism and turning inwards toward the comfort and fun inherent in the obviously good times. Symbolically, news of this turn was spread across the land by radio, the latest in modern technological entertainment. Westinghouse did not miss a beat as it began the nation's first regularly scheduled broadcasts, usually of live music, on KDKA.[12]

The marketing worked. Westinghouse joined the industrial triumvirate of GE, RCA, and AT&T. In the inevitable business shakeout, nonprofit organizations such as universities and churches failed or were bought out as the industrialists moved in. Federal regulation was needed and applied through the Federal Trade Commission and, in 1927, the new Federal Radio Commission. Herbert Hoover, the Secretary of

Commerce for much of the decade, worked hard to sort out the chaos. The Department had licensed 690 stations by the end of 1922. Americans spent $60 million on receiving gear in 1922. They bought 136 million radios in 1923. By 1924, their annual investment was $358 million.

Over their sets, fascinated Americans heard an eclectic mix of programs. Radio was initially a boon for the record industry. Most live music was classical. Jazz bands were not yet respectable or generally well enough known for the stations' audiences. Sporting events were popular from the beginning. As early as 1920, the Jack Dempsey-Georges Carpentier heavy-weight boxing championship and the New York Giants v. Yankees World Series had been broadcast. Calvin Coolidge became the first president to broadcast a State of the Union address on December 6, 1923. Cautious and cool Cal was also the first to have his inaugural address broadcast on March 4, 1925. Personalities emerged, the most notorious and financially successful being "Dr." John Brinkley, a shill who from KFKB in Milford, Kansas, sold elixirs and a goat-gland transplantation operation to increase potency.[13]

How could one not be interested in hearing the World Series, election results, Caruso, and Dr. Brinkley on goat glands? Certainly Nashville was not immune to the craze. Though the seductive impetus of the technology would have quickly entered the city anyway, it perhaps occurred earlier because Nashville had both one of the ubiquitous, gifted, pioneering radio hobbyists and a prescient businessman who recognized the potential profit in radio. The hobbyist was John Hibbett (Jack) DeWitt Jr. The businessman was Edwin Wilson Craig, Francis's first cousin. The stars of scientific inquiry and business acumen here crossed to the immeasurable benefit of Nashville, Tennessee—and Francis Craig.

While attending Duncan School, sixteen-year-old Jack DeWitt in 1922 created Nashville's first radio station, WDAA, at Ward-Belmont College. That June, he broadcast a Caruso record to the River and Rail Terminal downtown on the Cumberland River. He used the Victrola player of voice teacher Gaetano de Luca to send music over the twenty-watt transmitter.

The national burgeoning of radio stations was fantastic. This premier Nashville station was the nation's 275th, 181 of which had come on line between March and May that year. In 1923, Jack began commercial station WABC from his home. Bandleaders Francis Craig and Beasley Smith broadcast from the family living room through a transmitter in a converted chicken shed in the backyard.

DeWitt attended Vanderbilt University but left sometime in his sophomore year, much to the chagrin of his family, which had a proud history at the school. His father had been tapped for Phi Beta Kappa honors at Vanderbilt, and his uncle had won the Founder's Medal in the Medical School. Jack was just too obsessed with radio and felt he had nothing to learn at the university. He was probably right. His subsequent career included research at the Bell Laboratories, critical work on radar during World War II, and leadership of the project that first bounced a radar signal off the moon in 1946. While still at Vanderbilt, the genius tinkerer DeWitt helped build transmitters for station WSM, which would become the strongest station in the upper South and one of the most powerful in the nation. He would later serve as chief engineer and president of the station.[14]

Edwin Wilson Craig was born in Giles County in 1893, the first of C. A. and Maggie Craig's two children. He attended Tarbox and Wallace Schools in Nashville and Branham and Hughes Preparatory School in Spring Hill, Tennessee. He was a trendsetter in several ways for several Craig males. First, he loved and played music. At Branham and Hughes, he plucked mandolin in a band that included prominent Nashvillians Hugh Morgan and the Douglas boys, Beverly and Byrd. That hot group also featured a local Negro man playing lard stand bass. Second, he attended Vanderbilt and joined Phi Delta Theta.[15] Third, he never got his degree from the university. Last, most Craig men, including in-laws, had a go at the family insurance business. Ed dropped out of Vanderbilt in 1913 to sell "ordinary" insurance in Dallas for National Life.[16]

Edwin came back to the home office in 1920. By 1922, he was a vice president and in charge of the industrial department. Sometime prior to that, he had become interested in radio.

Unlike Jack DeWitt, his interest was principally nontechnical. Rather, he was a ham radio hobbyist, station listener, and participant in the informal, fluid relationship that developed between announcers and their audiences. He regularly fired off telegrams to the most popular announcers around the South, including George Hay while he was at WMC in Memphis.

Shortly after he returned to Nashville though, Ed decided that National Life should get into the radio business. The idea may have sprung from his close observation of WDAF in Kansas City and conversations with that station's management. When the insurance business frequently required his presence in Kansas City, Ed began visiting the station manager, Mr. Leo J. Fitzpatrick, the "Merry Old Chief." Though his motive may have been the pleasure of participation in a new technological adventure, he sold the idea to his father and the rest of the company board as a method of providing public service and good will (read "advertising") for the insurance company. He envisioned the station's message as a broadcasting bridge between the company's field men and their clients.[17]

Apparently none of the National Life hierarchy initially shared Edwin's enthusiasm for radio. President C. A. approved the project in order to keep his energetic son in company management. Edwin had threatened to resign and independently pursue a radio career, so the company gave him a "toy" station, WSM, in order to keep him on board. Whatever their motivation, the cash rich insurance company pursued the project in a first-class fashion with an initial investment of $50,000. In the South, the station's one-thousand-watt power was exceeded only by Atlanta's WSB. National Life built two plush studios on the fifth floor of its spanking new Seventh Avenue headquarters building, which had been dedicated only in 1924.[18]

WSM stood for We Shield Millions. This derived from words within the company's trademark, designed in 1922 and consisting of a shield on which was inscribed "The National Life and Accident Insurance Company, Incorporated, Shields You." If company leaders had been initially ambivalent about the radio venture, the station tag showed that they had at least begun to accept E. W.'s vision that this new medium might be a marketing tool. Despite continual touting of the station's service role, critical decisions about its management and direction would always be based on hardheaded business criteria. Management's acquiescence was to be real good for National Life.

The station's grand opening was the Monday evening of October 5, 1925. This followed a broadcast test the previous day in which a vocal selection by Miss Bonnie Barnhardt and two piano solos by Mr. Jack Keefe had been broadcast to Atlanta, using a frequency of 650 kilocycles (or kilohertz) and a wave length of 282.8 meters. WSM was to share that wave length for a short time with an already established station in Lawrenceburg, Tennessee. Secretary of Commerce Herbert Hoover, the "commissioner of radio," had wired the good news that the test had been successful.

Because demand for seats at the dedication far exceeded those available in the studios, loudspeakers were used to broadcast the proceedings to those packing Seventh Avenue. Master of Ceremonies George D. Hay, then at station WLS in Chicago, used his famous boat whistle to garner attention. After an invocation by Dr. James I. Vance of the First Presbyterian Church, C. A. Craig called the station the "Voice of the Athens of the South" and dedicated it to public service. Mayor Hilary House and Governor Austin Peay completed the solemnities with appropriate political benedictions.

Then the entertainment began. Considering WSM's future programming fame, there was a notable total absence of folk or "country" acts. Among those sending their music through the receptive Middle Tennessee air in the first hour were a vocal quintet from Fisk University and Beasley Smith's orchestra, heard by wire from the nearby Andrew Jackson Hotel. The long night was ended by the second band on the program, "Francis Craig's orchestra and their latest jazz." Craig's section was broadcast from his bandstand at the Hermitage Hotel and was called " . . . a grand jamboree of popular music in the most modern manner."

Following completion of the scheduled program, both orchestras' musicians retired to the National Life Building, and a huge party was held through the wee hours on the fourth and fifth floors. On hearing his son's music over the airways, Father Craig was said to have softened his disapproval of Francis's work choice. The young man's good music made people happy, and he was participating in a modern miracle. As was the case so often throughout his career, he was also in the right place at the right time.[19]

A SWEET AND SUCCESSFUL MUSICIAN

Father Craig's comfortable pride in Francis's quickly established reputation in Nashville and the mid-South was appropriate. In associating himself with WSM from its inception, the young man had completed the tripod on which his career would firmly rest. There were the regular hours and certain income accruing from his engagement as the house orchestra leader at the Hermitage Hotel. There was the incalculable benefit of broadcasting from the most powerful radio station in Tennessee to a regional population who were hungrily buying radio sets. From these two jobs sprang the publicity which resulted in the last leg of a balanced and busy career, the high society demand for Francis Craig and His Orchestra. Colleges, clubs, and cute southern coeds wanted to dance to his music. In a flush economic era, Craig had all the business he needed.

The orchestra's style evolved from the necessity to make a living and from Craig's personality and capability. He played what his particular public wanted. He had not only left behind the frivolities of youth, he seemed to have repressed any remnant of them. If there ever had been a tug between the unfettered, adventuresome life of a jazz musician and the staid, restricted adulthood a preacher father might admire, the forces of responsibility had obviously carried the day. The young breadwinner took seriously his several opportunities, working long hours to fulfill his contracts and care for his family.

In so doing, he seemed more like a buttoned-up professional than the stereotypical bandleader. Those who knew him must have recognized certain personality quirks that became increasingly apparent to his audiences. While the band might venture into enough new tunes and rhythms to satisfy the crowds, its leader's persona did not respond in sync. Francis was not a live wire on the stage or in front of a microphone. From the beginning he was reserved, almost aloof. One who recalled his performance style said he was "just there."

Though often pictured with a baton in publicity pictures, he rarely used the stick. He unobtrusively conducted with a hand (the other might be in his coat pocket) and alternately looked at the audience or the players, occasionally glaring at mistake makers. The contradiction between persona and profession was exemplified by the observation of a young man who enjoyed dancing to the orchestra's strains. As he watched Francis stand to the side of the piano and stolidly conduct, the maestro would suddenly break into a few bars of a joyful soft-shoe routine. Though the feet jumped, his face remained expressionless. A visceral, innate rhythm had apparently erupted through an increasingly dense, upper-class shell. Such actions were impromptu, unseen by the majority of the customers, and not done for their benefit. Though adept at relating to individuals, before large audiences he had the performance personality of an automaton. Any success he might earn would clearly have to come from his product and not his showmanship.[20]

In spite of the decade's reputation for adventure and iconoclasm, popular musicians in the twenties did not neces-sarily choose to pursue jazz if they wanted to make a living. An orchestra leader generally had to decide whether to go in a sweet or swinging direction. The choice was perhaps never that stark, and some groups did both well. Francis's tastes and those of his customers dictated that his orchestra's catalogue would consist largely of demure numbers. Just as he was not a tie-loosened, hard-drinking, experimenting, speakeasy player, his chosen audiences usually wanted orderly, soothing, usually danceable numbers. He had to satisfy Belle Meade professionals and debutantes more than any big-city nightclubbers out on the town. This was the Bible Belt, not Harlem's Cotton Club. Both Francis and his demographic targets swung very cautiously.

Diners at the Hermitage certainly did not want their conversations or digestion disrupted by upbeat noise. Early in his marriage and employment at the hotel, Francis wrote a beautiful ballad that would become his theme song and, until 1947, be the tune most associated with his orchestra. While enjoying a Birmingham vacation in spring 1928, Francis admired some blooming red roses. He must have been in a romantic mood, as he quickly penned "Red Rose" in honor of Elizabeth.[21] The dreamy, sweet song would open countless radio and dinner performances for the next two decades. During that same time, customers at the Grill Room would enjoy a veritable trademark single red rose in a bud vase on each pristine, linen-covered table. Craig's soft music and familiar, genteel conversation with those seated around the red roses were central to the classy dining experience at the Hermitage.

Things continued to go well for Francis at WSM. The yield for him was not in salary but in the airway publicity by which the orchestra became known beyond Nashville. In a time of relatively uncluttered airways, the station signal reached a long way, providing a new and then immeasurable boast to performers and products. Francis's niece, Mary Elizabeth, remembered tediously twirling her radio dial in Florida and proudly listening with her pals to her kinsman's performance.

Initially there was no daytime broadcasting. A dinner concert from the nearby hotels began at 6:30 P.M.—a secure slot for "Cu'n" (as his relatives pronounced it) Francis Craig. A couple of hours of music by local

"Red Rose" sheet music cover.

singers or instrumentalists began at 10:00 P.M. Performers included the Fisk Jubilee singers and talent from Nashville's colleges and universities, Ward-Belmont, Peabody, Vanderbilt. Almost all this abbreviated programming was classical or semi-classical. Management's initial effort may have reflected their own highbrow taste, but they would soon accommodate their less polished listening public with some real popular lowbrow material.

After participating in WSM's opening broadcast, George D. Hay had been persuaded by management to stay in Nashville as the station's radio director. He assumed that job in early November. Less than two months after the station opened, he featured Uncle Jimmy Thompson, a popular, regional, folk fiddler, on a November 28, 1925, broadcast. Because of the huge audience response to that broadcast and his own inclinations about programming, Hay decided to begin a WSM Barn Dance, similar to the WLS Barn Dance he had instituted in Chicago. Hay coined a historic label on December 10, 1927, when he called the *Barn Dance* the *Grand Old* (later designated *Ole*) *Opry*. In addition to Uncle Jimmy, initial stars (perhaps a grandiose designation) included Uncle Dave Macon, Dr. Humphrey Bate and his 'Possum Hunters, Sam and Kirk McGee, and DeFord Bailey, "a little hunchback colored boy" harmonica player. Nashville radio programming would never be the same, as the *Opry*

Opening Saturday

MAY THE ELEVENTH

The **HERMITAGE GRILL ROOM**

•

With

Francis Craig's Orchestra

•

Featuring delicious foods, tastily served, in an atmosphere that lends itself to good cheer.

BREAKFAST   LUNCHEON   DINNER

The HERMITAGE
HOTEL GRILL ROOM

Advertisement for the Hermitage Grill Room.

began what was to become the longest continuous running live radio show in the United States.[22]

WSM was now totally committed to surviving in the new world of communication competition. Though anticipating future profit from insurance sales, National Life lost an average of almost $70,000 per year during the station's first decade. In 1926, WSM joined the National Broadcasting System, the first nationwide network. This provided local access to the network's best programs and national exposure for the station's own talent. WSM increased its power to 5,000 watts in 1927 and was given a band of 890 kilocycles. A truly significant distinction and broadcasting benefit came in 1928, when the Federal Radio Commission made it one of forty national "clear channel" stations—at 650 kilocycles, the spot on the radio dial which the public quickly came to identify as WSM's. The clear channel allowed the station to broadcast without interference to supposedly underserved, rural areas.[23] WSM was a powerful broadcasting axle in a big wheel of the rural, agricultural upper South. The clear channel capability enhanced the station's business and strongly influenced its programming. What could possibly be more interesting to farm families than the *Grand Old Opry*? Might those listeners also be interested in buying some industrial insurance?

Francis Craig seemed energized by his several opportunities and was willing to work. In addition to the hotel, radio, and weekend dance engagements, his orchestra made several recordings for Columbia Records in Atlanta. On January 27, 1925, the group recorded "Marble Halls" and "Steady Roll Blues," which Columbia rejected. Their work must have improved, for eight months later the company released recordings of these two songs as well as "Mighty Lak' A Rose" and "Forgiveness." There were also sessions followed by releases in April 1926, and April 1928. "Red Rose" was recorded for the first time on the last date (discography).[24]

The recorded songs were ballads or novelty tunes with a regional flavor. Francis's meager publicity was always provincial, emphasizing his orchestra's southern origin and product. A reviewer of "Steady Roll Blues" and "Marble Halls" exulted that, "These selections give the Southern boys ample opportunity to display the real Southern style of fox trot that has made them so popular with the young folks in their vicinity." A rhythm section of tuba, guitar, piano, and drums (with prominent high-hat cymbals) underlay brass and reed melody makers playing in a random, Dixieland manner. There were no arrangement innovations, and the music could be best described as 1920s cute and catchy. Fans of Francis Craig and his predominantly sweet later style would have never recognized the music as his.

Craig had not been especially excited about the recording opportunity. His lack of enthusiasm was appropriate. Radio was cutting into rather than enhancing the record business nationally, and sales at the end of the decade would be much less than the peak year of 1921. Royalties were a fantasy, as performers were then paid a flat rate per four-side session. There was not a moneymaker in the bandleader's lot, although "Steady Roll Blues" was a "Hit of the Month." He could at least market his operation as "Francis Craig and His Columbia Recording Orchestra." He did not expect to record more unless "someone asked him."[25]

Craig's orchestras always had excellent musicians. He recognized talent, and the better players wanted to be in his employ. There were several reasons for this. Performers migrated to Nashville hoping to work on WSM and thus advance their careers. Craig's relationship to the important radio station was well-known. More important, though, was the high quality of his orchestra's work. He had a very good group. Though his music was predictable and non-innovative, it was done well. The orchestra leader ran a tight ship and had plenty of business.

From the beginning of his career, one of the prevailing features of Craig's band was the quality of its "graduates," that is, orchestra members who went on to important careers of their own. Though Francis may not have intended it, their work with him was effectively a minor league experience, which prepared them for the big leagues. Much of his ultimately national reputation sprang from the association of former employees with his orchestra.

The rosters of the Atlanta recording sessions included some who would make names for themselves in the popular music world. Two who would become quite well known were Kenny Sargent and James (Jimmy) Melton. Both were singers and reed men, providing talent versatility most helpful to a tightly budgeted operation. Sargent would become a saxophonist and featured vocalist for Glen Gray and the Casa Loma Orchestra in the early 1930s. Melton would become a movie and radio star and sing tenor with the Metropolitan Opera![26]

"To Francis and Elizabeth with warmest personal regards, James Melton, 6-8-'27." (Courtesy of Donia Craig Dickerson)

With all this activity, Craig's widow still recalled the most consistently predictable business came from Saturday night dances at the Belle Meade Country Club, where he was as familiar as the club's "greens and sandtraps."[28] All the reputation gained from radio and hotel work had to be cashed in at dance parties. Such work required his music be rhythmic and danceable but also noncontroversial and unspectacular. Musical experimentation and virtuosity were unnecessary and might have alienated his audience. Though most of them were good professionals, none of his players had to emulate Jack Teagarden or Bix Beiderbecke. Francis did not need and would not pay any such standout in the band. It would help business if his orchestra could approach the quality of groups led by Eddie Duchin, Anson Weeks, and Shep Fields, the rising metropolitan society orchestras of the day. Actually, they did. Once or twice most weekends, Francis Craig and His Orchestra played dances for the Cotillion Club, country clubs, or debuts. They *were* Nashville's society orchestra.

As the decade of the 1920s wound down, the frenetic tempo
of American life only increased. President Coolidge reassured
that the business of America was business. In 1927, Al Jolson
sang "Mammy" in *The Jazz Singer*. That same year, the ultimate
American hero, Charles Lindbergh, returned safely from France
to huzzahs from a worshipful generation. In September 1929,
RCA stock peaked at $114\frac{3}{4}$, a rise of 600 percent in eighteen
months. Americans danced, sang, invested, drank, listened to
their radios and records, and, in general, just enjoyed life. Surely
this would go on forever.[28]

The pace of Francis Craig's career was moving in lockstep
with that of the nation's. He now had the added responsibility of
a family. His first child, daughter Lazynka Celeste, was born on
Valentine's Day 1929. (She hated her first name and never used
it.) In seeking security for his young family, the dutiful Francis
was working very hard and making good, not great, money.
There was no immediate indication that the Francis Craigs
would be hurt by the stock market crash of October 1929. They
had not invested significantly in equities. Few noneconomists
foresaw the imminent depression. Francis was still multiply
employed. What's more, he was at the very top of his game.

In marketing its third annual radio show in summer 1928,
on which the bands of Francis Craig, Charles Domberger (of
Atlantic City), and Vito Pellettieri were to be featured, the
Nashville Banner called the twenty-eight-year-old Francis "one of
the youngest orchestra leaders today. . . . " His radio
orchestra, the Rhythm Symphony, held down the choice dinner
slot, 6:30–7:00 P.M. on WSM's now thirteen-hour broadcast day.

The band's excellent product was well-known, and Francis
dealt from strength in selling it—all from a "little black book"
he carried in his pocket. He continued to play dates at colleges
and dance emporia all over the South—Tampa, Sarasota, and
Ocala, Florida; the Cinderella Garden in Little Rock, Arkansas;
and a several-week summer 1929 engagement at the Park Lake
Hollywood Barn in Lansing, Michigan.

Perhaps to get a better deal, he left the friendly and secure
confines of the Hermitage in 1929 to work for its principle
competition, the Andrew Jackson Hotel, a block away on Sixth

Francis Craig and His Andrew Jackson Hotel Orchestra

September 16–23, 1929, issue of Nashville This Week.

Avenue and Deaderick Street. The hotel headlined the announcement of the arrangement by calling his the "Best All-round Orchestra in (the) South." He signed a two-year contract there similar to the one he had enjoyed at the Hermitage—playing lunch ("Andrew Jackson Hotel Luncheon Concert") and dinner ("Francis Craig and his Andrew Jackson Hotel Orchestra") throughout the week, with most shows being broadcast on WSM. This bandstand had been occupied by Beasley Smith through 1927 and Vito Pellettieri in 1928.[30]

In April 1930, Francis Craig's band won a popularity contest among *Nashville Banner* readers as the most popular local radio feature. Runners-up among listeners included the

Golden Art Hour, Christine Lamb, and the National Concert Orchestra. The *Grand Ole Opry* finished *sixth*. Either the *Opry* had not approached the popularity it would later enjoy, or *Banner* readers had quite different tastes from the rest of the radio audience. After hearing paeans about his "enduring and growing" popularity at the presentation program, Francis's group played "The Sweetheart of Sigma Chi," because several *Banner* staff members had been members of that fraternity. This panoply of success and apparently endless business occurred before he was thirty years old.[30]

Though Francis Craig did not carouse, drank very sparingly, and used no illicit drugs to which modern pop musicians seemed susceptible, he did smoke heavily, beginning before breakfast and continuing through long nights of work. Everyone attributed the young man's persistent cough to that socially acceptable habit. His wife believed some weight loss that spring—he was down to 142 pounds—and progressive fatigue were due to not eating right and overwork, which Francis was clearly doing.

As he worked through the usual round of seasonal proms, he began coughing up blood. Depictors of his hemoptysis (expectoration of blood) painted numerous dramatic pictures of the frightening phenomenon. Bowen Ingram described the discreet hacking of a bit of bloody spittle into his handkerchief while he was doing a radio broadcast. Elizabeth Romine said he hemorrhaged onto the keyboard during a dance engagement.

His wife recalled Francis fainted while participating in a rehearsal for Vanderbilt's Cap and Bells. This was a musical review produced by students, faculty, and graduates that was performed in the spring and then taken on tour through the upper South. Francis had participated in the first such musicale in 1929, scoring the music and directing the orchestra. On top of all his other obligations, he was working hard on the 1930 review. Andrew Lytle, a young member of the Vanderbilt Agrarians and friend of Craig's, was also a trained dramatist and helped direct the 1930 show, entitled "Let's Go." After hearing of Francis's illness, Lytle worried he had worked him too hard, thereby causing him to break down.[31]

Regardless of the varying literary versions of his illness, Francis Craig was real sick. His physician, Dr. John Owsley Manier, informed him that he had tuberculosis. The good doctor's diagnostic criteria are unknown, but his opinion was unequivocal. The treatment was immediate cessation of work and admission to a sanitarium. Francis Craig's career was, at least, on hold. As the nation plunged into the Depression, his own economic future was, euphemistically, tenuous. More important, he was afflicted with a dangerous, potentially fatal disease. The Red Rose had suddenly and unexpectedly lost its bloom.

An obscure paragraph in a mid-May newspaper radio column noted that Craig's orchestra would play its usual late Sunday evening *Rhythm Symphony* slot despite its leader's confinement at home because of (unspecified) illness. Within a couple of weeks of getting a check for $250 for the band's playing at the Nashville Cotillion Club spring dance, Francis Craig was in Colorado receiving the best contemporary treatment for tuberculosis. He did not know when or if he would be getting any more such payments for orchestra work well done.[32]

CHAPTER THREE

There's just one place for me, NEAR YOU.

larghetto poco a poco

Slow, Little by Little

The security and future expectations of twenty-nine-year-old Francis Craig and his family were sorely threatened by the acute onset of his pulmonary tuberculosis in the spring of 1930. A booming regional career as a popular dance bandleader seemed about to ride the mysterious waves of radio and recording to national prominence. There seemed no reason why Francis could not become known as an American maestro instead of just a southern one.[1] He had enough ambition, a huge capacity for work, and a proven ability to hire and manage a sweet society orchestra, one that would be in steady demand.

Now though, he was to be packed off into indefinite isolation from those he loved in an attempt to arrest the course of a potentially fatal disease. He had a one-year-old daughter, a mortgage, and modest savings. Though Mrs. Gewin, Elizabeth's mother, was capable of helping with both shelter and money, Francis Craig was by no means wealthy.[2] His personal jeopardy was compounded by a looming threat to the economic and political stability of the United States—the Great Depression. Craig's life had descended from youthful, almost precocious, zenith to ominous nadir in the short time it took to expectorate a bloody glob of tubercle bacilli-laced sputum.

THE WHITE PLAGUE

Though there is evidence that tuberculosis (consumption, phthisis, TB, the white plague) was an ancient disease, it became the most important public health threat in the world only after the onset of the nineteenth-century industrial revolution. The urbanization of society resulted in crowded, unsanitary conditions ideal for the spread of the disease, mainly by the sputum vehicle broadcast by those infected with the (usual) pulmonary variant of the disease. Francis Craig certainly worked in close crowds.

Tuberculosis was the most common infectious disease in the world from approximately the mid-nineteenth to the mid-twentieth centuries. A prevalent statistic during that time was that untreated patients would experience a 50 percent mortality rate within five years of contracting the disease. In the eastern United States in the early nineteenth century, the mortality rate for tuberculosis was 400/100,000 population. Death came from inanition (loss of vitality), toxicity, or, most dramatically, hemorrhage from the lungs. Victims minimally faced debility, fever, and pain. Even those who survived the acute illness faced the possibility of its later recurrence. Though Robert Koch had isolated the tubercle bacillus in 1882, physicians simply had no way to kill the organism. Tuberculosis was responsible for one-seventh of deaths worldwide by the end of the nineteenth century. In 1930, it was still a potent killer. The TB death rate in the United States was 71.1 per 100,000 population, a rate trailing only cardiovascular disease, influenza and pneumonia, and malignant neoplasms.

Most Americans associated TB with poor immigrants crowded into eastern tenement slums, but it was prevalent in the more rural open spaces of the nation—such as Tennessee. It was also no respecter of class. The disease cut a wide swath through Francis Craig's family and the upper crust of Nashville. His grandfather, William Jackson Craig, had died of consumption. His uncle, C. A., had spent some six months in a sanitarium in 1915–1916. His fraternity brother and increasingly recognized poet, Allen Tate, had been exiled in the North Carolina mountains for nine months in 1922, just as he was completing college. Closer to home, Elizabeth's father, Dr. Gewin, had died of TB in an Asheville, North Carolina, sanitarium in July 1929, less than a year before Francis was diagnosed. Dr. Alfred Blalock was a rising star at the new Vanderbilt Medical Center and later was chairman of the Department of Surgery at Johns Hopkins and co-inventor of the revolutionary "blue baby" operation. Beginning in 1927, he had been confined for a year at the most famous of all United States tuberculosis hospitals, the Trudeau Sanatorium in Saranac Lake, New York.[3]

Antibacterial therapy for tuberculosis was not available until the discovery of streptomycin in 1943. So, treatment was essentially the same as that propounded in Germany in the latter half of the previous century, quarantine in an institution. Thus was the victim of a killer communicable disease kept away from the supposedly unafflicted. Treatment received at tuberculosis hospitals varied and depended on conflicting, often unscientific theories. The treating physician at one institution might recommend strict rest because decreased lung activity supposedly allowed the infectious organisms to be sequestered. Mild exercise, perhaps at a higher altitude, might be used at another facility because increased metabolism made the heart work faster, thereby more rapidly clearing the system of infection. Two therapy tenets accepted by most were the benefits of fresh air (the colder the better) and stuffing patients with calories, as much as five thousand per day.[4]

Authors and composers imbued consumption with a romantic aura throughout much of its prevalence. Consider Mimi in Puccini's *La Boheme*, Hans Castorp in Thomas Mann's *The Magic Mountain*, or Alexander Dumas's *Camille*. With time and the observation of the disease's ravages though, the disease evolved in public perception and literary depiction from exotic to dirty and degrading. Consider Ratso Rizzo in *Midnight Cowboy*. There was no romance for the victim. In addition to physical suffering and possible death, victims faced the stigma of contamination and the loneliness of treatment or societal isolation. These figurative lepers self-deprecatingly called themselves "tbs" or "lungers."

Patients' egos were further destroyed by sanitarium regime. Mind manipulation through the repetition of ubiquitous optimistic aphorisms was a big part of most treatment programs, yet unhappiness and despair were the usual patient moods. First, there was the uncertainty of prognosis. Twenty-five percent of hospitalized patients died, and 50 percent of released patients died within five years. It was difficult to enthusiastically embrace treatment routines that were rigid, restrictive, and depressing. Assuming no surgical therapy, a typical day consisted of four meals, considerable supine rest, very limited exercise, frequent temperature assessment, and periodic weighing, a frightening ordeal that quantified cure or deterioration. This unfulfilled existence might go on for years.

Of course conditions were better for those with money than for those without. The poor inhabited crowded state institutions or, if ostracized, might live in tent cities outside isolated, usually western United States towns. The wealthy might be treated in truly cushy conditions with exotic foods and plentiful staff. Still, whatever one's net worth, TB treatment was usually a lonely, frightening, degrading experience.[5]

Within a few days of learning his diagnosis, Francis Craig traveled by train to The Oakes Home in Denver, Colorado. That sanitarium was chosen because his uncle, C. A., had been treated there. Letters of encouragement and concern began immediately. Mary Webb Haggard of the Vanderbilt Registrar's Office wrote to express joy over hearing he was feeling better and to praise his "saintly" father and mother. Father Craig reminded him of God's love. "Rest, and with trust in God, gain strength as the days go by."[6]

The Oakes Home was commodious and warm. Named after Episcopal Rev. Frederick W. Oakes, it was founded in 1895 and was said to be the second sanitarium in the United States. The big, colonial main building had numerous fireplaces, a large library, artesian water, and workshops. Rates were twenty-one to twenty-five dollars per week for private rooms. Perhaps someone confined for tuberculosis could never conclude he was residing in a resort, but the Oakes Home simulated that in appearance and amenities. There were worse places to take the cure.[7]

The Oakes Home in Denver, Colorado. (Photo by L. C. McClure, courtesy of Denver Public Library, Western History Department)

Little is recorded about Francis's treatment in Denver. Except for isolation from society, his regimen was apparently not excessively restrictive or oppressive. It consisted of rest, plenty of exposure to the mile-high air, and much food, including superb venison at Christmas. He took no medicine, "not even an aspirin."

Yet another afflicted member of his Nashville set befriended Francis at the Oakes. Homer Gibbs was two years younger than Francis and had Potts disease, tuberculosis of the spine. He was an employee of the mortgage loan department of National Life, and C. A. Craig had also recommended the Oakes Home to him. Though he and Francis were not close before or after their confinements, they supported each other during the long months in Denver.

Francis's wife had a long visit with him that autumn, leaving little Celeste with her recently widowed Grandmother Gewin in Birmingham. Francis's parents continued to reside in the Whitland Avenue home. Elizabeth Craig Lancaster remembered that the family's financial condition was "rough." They got by with the aid of their parents and some money her young husband had set aside. "He was a great saver."[8]

The orchestra continued to satisfy their dance contracts. They toured most of that summer 1930. Under the interim leader, trombonist Bradford Smith, they played jobs in St. Louis (Chase Hotel), Kansas City (Muehlebach Hotel), and Dallas, cashing in on Francis Craig's growing reputation throughout the South and Midwest. They were back in Nashville for the opening of fall term at Vanderbilt, further enhancing their reputation as the most popular orchestra on the campus.[9]

Francis apparently did no musical work during his confinement. He was not depressed and saw his confinement as just something he had to endure. He seemed impervious to the usual therapeutic trauma felt by most patients. His mood was reflective and upbeat as he penned a Christmas poem to his parents from Colorado. He seemed intent on recovery and returning to his profession:

A fight I've fought against the wall,
Yet through it all I've heard your call;
I shall live, and breathe, and sing a song,
'Tis you to whom my songs belong.[10]

Sometime "after the weather got warm" in 1931, Francis Craig returned to Nashville. His confinement-treatment had lasted one year. Elizabeth noted he had excellent color and energy. The most striking change was his relative corpulence. He now packed over 180 pounds on his formerly lanky frame. "He could hardly get out of the car." She did not notice any special emotional change. He was neither more pessimistic nor optimistic than before he got sick. He seemed the same as before. Craig was apparently not susceptible to mood swings. His impassive demeanor reflected a fatalistic attitude toward life's vicissitudes. It was, if possible, now time to restart their lives. Francis approached that task with equanimity and purpose.[10]

ON WITH THE SHOW—A MIDLIFE RALLY

Before Francis could renew his career as a bandleader, he needed a band. Though most of the musicians who had been playing with him in 1930 were still available, they were unsure just who their boss was. Bradford Smith had led the group, apparently reasonably well. Succumbing to opportunism, he tried to convince the musicians that they were better off with him waving the baton than Francis Craig. Some of the boys believed him. Whose orchestra was it?

Beyond his orchestra work, Francis Craig had a passive attitude toward life. In addition to Elizabeth, he fortunately had a coterie of loyal, influential friends who usually came to his rescue in times of trouble, sometimes even without his requesting aid. To get rid of his new nemesis, Francis called on one of the men who over the years acted as "quasi guardians" for him, lawyer friend Ferris Bailey.[12]

It was clear that Francis did not own the musicians, and their contract with him was rather loose. Their obligations were to themselves. However, Francis did have clear title to the large and valuable music library the orchestra used. After Bailey clarified the conundrum, the boys in the band knew to whom their allegiance was owed. This was the Depression; they needed employment. The palace *coup d'etat* had been squelched. Exit Mr. Smith; enter Mr. Craig. Now it was time to go to work.[13]

There seemed to be plenty of it via the proven venues—proms, radio, hotels. The "South's leading orchestra" headed back out in their car caravans to colleges and car shows, benefits and balls. WSM's Sunday evening *Rhythm Symphony* radio show welcomed back its original conductor. Before the end of 1931, Francis's orchestra made the allegedly first national broadcast from a "Southern" hotel via the NBC "red" network. True, the time slot of 12:30–1:00 A.M. was not a premium one, but this was a pretty gaudy feather in his career cap. Contrary to Francis's historic association with the Hermitage Hotel, the broadcast was made from the Andrew Jackson, with which he was still contracted after his return from the Oakes Home.[14]

Francis Craig may have used his Colorado confinement to contact western hotels, for in June 1932, he began his biggest and best tour with the orchestra. Though they later had a few brief distant engagements, they would never be gone from home so long as this—over half a year. This was not the classical bus-hopping, enervating schedule of one-nighters most bands played. Francis's was still a hotel orchestra that usually stayed put in one place.

It all began on June twenty-fifth with a three-month stand at the exclusive Broadmoor Hotel (Nite Club) in Colorado Springs. Francis had left Elizabeth in Birmingham with their second daughter, two-month-old Donia Frost. Characteristic of their usual hectic schedule, the band stayed busy. They played four hours, five nights per week for dinner and dancing. Continuing his promising relationship with NBC, Francis also had the orchestra broadcast nationally down the road in Denver three afternoons a week from local station KOA through WJZ in New York, NBC's "blue" network.

These broadcasts could be heard back home in Nashville and Birmingham. Because of Elizabeth's hometown prominence, the Birmingham papers paid considerable attention to her husband throughout his career. Stories on the Broadmoor engagement highlighted the three Birmingham boys in the band, Cecil Bailey, William Yandle, and Newt Richardson. It was also noted that the KOA announcer for his Denver radio program was Walter Campbell, a former Birmingham announcer (WAPI), who had worked with Craig at WSM.[15]

Clint Garvin was a young reed man who began almost a decade's work with Francis on this big western trip. He recalled the Broadmoor as being absolutely as classy as it got in 1932. Some suites supposedly went for one hundred dollars per night. The King of Siam was a guest that summer. The golf pro was the famous Bobby Thompson, whose wife was the alluring screen star Viola Dana. How much more glamorous could it get?

Francis Craig (far left) and his twelve-piece band. Left to right—*front row: Max Hart, guitar; Jimmy Gallagher, sax; Powell Adams, drums; Newt Richardson, sax; Red Cunningham, trumpet.* Middle row: *Tommy Harrison, trombone; Mickey Tennity, trumpet; Red Hawn, violin.* Back row: *John Gordy, piano; Clint Garvin, sax; Bill Yandle, bass. (From P. J. Broome and Clay Tucker,* The Other Music City, *1990)*

There was plenty of time for recreation. Detached from the crumbling outside world, the southerners basked in the idyllic comforts of a luxury hotel. A few wives accompanied the band members. The boys got to enjoy the gorgeous, championship golf course, something they would never have been able to otherwise afford. Everyone rode up Pikes Peak and generally enjoyed being a tourist.[16]

Craig received nice congratulatory notes about his Broadmoor work from, among others, Horace Heidt and Ted Lewis. He got some embarrassing publicity from an accident that typified his lifelong propensity to gaffes. While driving one midday, he became overcome by tear gas. The Colorado heat had apparently melted the paraffin in a tear gun he carried for protection in his closed auto, disabling the maestro.[17]

In September, the band went to Dallas for a six-week engagement at the Adolphus Hotel (Hollywood Dinner Club). Publicity material highlighted the crooning of trombonist Tommy Harrison and Clint Garvin, "specialist in negro songs." These were not sung in dialect. Rather they were jazz pieces, e.g., "Hobo, Don't Ride that Train," popularized by Negro musicians such as Louis Armstrong, one of Clint's heroes. While in the Big D, Craig hired Alpha Louise Morton, a fine vocalist soon to be billed as the "NBC Blues Singer." Again they broadcast nationally—over KRLD. That station's ten thousand watts allowed Nashvillians to hear Craig while Beasley Smith filled in at WSM.[18]

The briefest stop, ten days, was in San Antonio at the Gunter Hotel. Marketing for the engagement was Texas hokey. Francis declared "I am the son of a Methodist minister and I think music is good for the soul." His orchestra never had a permanent name, seeming to change monikers by the week. There was, though, a repetition of its southern origin, which it emphasized in its music and (occasional) humor. In San Antonio, they called themselves the "Band From the South." Publicity blurbs extolled the " . . . leisurely and dreamy quality which is the spirit of the Old South."

Finally, Francis and the orchestra moved back to Colorado, this time to Denver. The Cosmopolitan Hotel with much hoopla opened its new Silver Glade dance hall with the band from

Craig Gets the "Big Time" Contract

A smug Francis Craig, on top of his game.

Nashville on October fifteenth. "Never in the history of Denver's Night Life has there been an event so important or so colorful as the New Silver Glade's opening night." Well . . . !

Again no one could settle on a name. Within three months and depending on the performance locale, the band was called Francis Craig and His Serenaders, Francis Craig and His Band from the South, and Francis Craig and his All-Star Silver Glade Orchestra. Presumably they did not suffer an identity crisis as long as they were getting paid.

Francis enjoyed a fond taste of home at the Cosmopolitan. Elizabeth and little Celeste came out to live in the hotel with him. He also got to showcase the band's wares on a national broadcast that was auspicious for WSM. Under the supervision of its new chief engineer, Jack DeWitt, WSM increased its power to fifty thousand watts in November, making it as powerful as any other station in the nation. After a program from WSM to forty stations from 10:00–11:15 P.M., NBC broadcast a forty-five minute national program of congratulations, with segments from New York, Cleveland, Chicago, Denver, and San Francisco. Craig proudly headlined the Denver segment to Tennessee and the other forty-seven states.

The now twelve-piece orchestra and girl singer Alpha Louise Morton played at the Silver Glade through the lucrative winter holidays. A five-course Christmas dinner cost $1.50. Saturday dinners cost $2.50 per. A guest could dance for only $1.00. Charges were less during the week. The gala New Year's Eve dance cost a whopping $6.00 per celebrant.

The orchestra returned to Denver station KOA. Beginning in January 1933, they broadcast afternoon programs nationally through NBC's blue network. At every stop on the tour, Francis had arranged national dissemination of his orchestra's strains. He was all over this new and wonderful opportunity. His appeal to the network and growing national reputation were highlighted by the orchestra being one of four featured on NBC's national New Year's Eve "Dancing Across the Country" broadcast, December 31, 1932.[19]

Craig's musicians noted some socioeconomic contrasts on this trip. While they were working steadily for decent wages (around forty dollars per week) on the bandstand, the Depression was going on outside. In the big western crossroads-city of Denver, "bums" were all over the place. Whatever they thought about Francis Craig's personality (pleasant, but aloof) or music (pedestrian, but well done), he provided them steady work, a precious commodity in 1933. As they headed back to Nashville that February, the boys (and occasional girl) in the band looked respectfully upon their boss as a reliable meal ticket, a feature of their relationship to him that engendered musicians' loyalty. He got them jobs. Thus, Francis was able to attract the best players and vocalists. Because of the resultant consistent high quality, Francis Craig and what-ever his orchestra was called this week would invariably stay front and center, during bad times as well as good.[20]

HUNKERIN' DOWN

Just as Francis Craig began the 1930s with illness, his nation, state, and hometown faced huge problems in the new decade. By late 1932, stocks had crashed to 20 percent of their 1929 valuation. Spending and

Alpha Louise (later Kay) Morton.
(Courtesy of Marjorie Arnold Kirby)

production fell, and unemployment rose to over one quarter of the national work force. Eleven thousand banks had failed by 1933. The Great Depression was underway; and, despite President Roosevelt's obvious leadership strengths and a proliferation of alphabet-soup Federal agencies, there was no end to it in sight.[21]

Tennessee was poor and about to get poorer. In 1929, the per capita income in Tennessee was $375 per person. A nationwide drought in the early thirties hurt Tennessee farmers. Both yields and prices of cotton, corn, and tobacco plummeted. Money was neither being made nor spent. As poverty set in, only 11,696 new vehicles were registered to Tennesseans in 1932, down from 55,211 in 1929. By the end of 1933, over one-third of Tennessee's major industrial plants had closed.[22]

Nashville anticipated the Great Depression with a financial collapse of its own. The financial empire of Rogers Caldwell began teetering in 1929. A successful purveyor of southern bonds prior to World War I, he and his cohort Luke Lea had created a megalith of banks, insurance companies, commercial enterprises, even professional athletic teams throughout the South in the twenties. Properties were heavily mortgaged, and money was routinely kited. Their success depended on a questionable relationship between Caldwell's commercial businesses, his principle bank, the Bank of Tennessee, and the State of Tennessee and its compliant governor, Henry Horton. In complicated stages, the insolvent empire disintegrated along with one hundred twenty banks in seven states in November, 1930. Though Nashville had a financial infrastructure which would return to vitality in a couple of decades, "The Wall Street of the South" seemed only an evanescent dream as the Depression settled in.[23]

Though bad enough, the Depression would not be as bad in Nashville and other southern cities as in the North, which was more dependent on industrial wage labor. Nashville's unemployment rate by 1934 peaked at "only" 13 percent. These relatively less stark conditions showed in public and journalistic perceptions of the crisis. Nashvillians, whose economy depended more on commerce and finance, were generally less anxious than their brethren from other sections, though moods varied depending upon whose ox was being gored.[24]

The entertainment business was inevitably affected by the downturn, though not as much as others. The recording industry had been on the skids since the advent of popular radio. That descent was accelerated by the Depression. Record sales were off 40 percent in 1932 from the previous year. Moviemakers cut back by, among other measures, sending back east many of the musicians they had enticed to the West Coast in a fatter time. Radio was not hurt so much. There were plenty of sets out there, and advertisers identified enough buyers to warrant their investment in the medium.[25]

All was not gloom and doom in the band business. Changes were afoot that would boost Francis Craig just as he entered the fullest decade of his career. Beginning late in the twenties, Fletcher Henderson led the breakaway from both the staid orchestrations of Paul Whiteman and the meanderings of

Francis Craig and his band at the Cosmopolitan Hotel, Denver, 1932. (Courtesy of Donia Craig Dickerson)

Dixieland music. With innovative arrangements, his big band of excellent musicians played from charts but also featured extemporized jazz solos. There was an apparent lull in the evolution of big bands as the Depression set in. The public was in no mood for change and momentarily preferred crooners, e.g., Bing Crosby, and sweet bands, e.g. Guy Lombardo, Jan Garber, and Wayne King, to whose band Francis's would frequently be compared.

That temporary pause was ended by the innovations of, among others, Glen Gray and Benny Goodman, the "King of Swing." Gray and his Casa Loma Orchestra, featuring Francis's former saxist and vocalist Kenny Sargent, were a versatile group. Their jazz flavor was prevalent enough to approach what would soon officially be designated swing; but they also remained a dance orchestra, producing some of the best ballad sounds yet. Fletcher Henderson as arranger had much to do with the impact of Goodman's first big band, formed in 1934.

There is disagreement about just when the Big Band era officially began. Two events in 1935 were worthy designees to be such a milestone. The Casa Loma Orchestra played a boffo concert at the Paramount Theater in New York, demonstrating that such music was suitable for listening as well as dancing. That same year, Camel cigarettes sponsored "Let's Dance," a coast-to-coast Saturday night program featuring Benny Goodman. As other cigarette companies subsequently sponsored other great bands (Glen Miller, Artie Shaw, Tommy Dorsey, Harry James, et al.), a more optimistic America reveled in the exuberance, romance, and fine musicianship of the genre. Once more, Francis Craig's table was being set by fortuitous circumstance. Once more, he had the energy and capability of feasting from that board.[26]

So how would things go for Craig as he returned from his triumphal tour of the West? Quite well, thank you. There seemed enough money from all the previous buyers of his music, and more as well. There would be no more big tours, and the band had to show up for work. However, there was plenty of that. Their experience was not to be that of the big moneymakers such as Glenn Miller or Tommy Dorsey, but it was to be far from a soup line. Both he and his players had plenty of income during the thirties. Observed Clint Garvin, "He never saw a Depression."[27] Francis Craig and his players cashed steady paychecks by staying busy. With their frantic pace, they sometimes seemed to refute a basic law of physics, apparently being in two places at once.

Francis settled on an orchestral instrumentation that he would use for the balance of his career. Gradually eliminating along the way the tuba, banjo, and violin, he used four saxophones (with clarinet capability), four brass (three trumpets and a trombone), and a rhythm section of piano, string bass, and drums.[28] There were no gimmicks here.

Vandy students welcomed Francis back with open arms and jumpy feet. They were eager to "shake a leg with Francis Craig." He played the big junior prom and multiple campus fraternity and sorority parties that early spring. The 1933 yearbook extended *"merci boucoup"* to their favorite band-leader for his work on the campus. Ever loyal to Phi Delta

stall of fame

All of you will have a date on
The night this master of the baton
Coaxes rhythms hot and sweet
To animate your dancing feet.
If you don't know him, take it from
Us you'll see him at the Prom.

Craig caricature in Vanderbilt Masquerader.

Theta, Craig usually gave his old frat a price break, sometimes playing four-hour dances for $90. The usual price was $150.

All his former Nashville customers—high school fraternities, Belle Meade Country Club, the Cotillion Club—still wanted his services. Between 1924 and 1946, Craig's group

played seven Bachelor's Club annual dances, more than twice
as many as any other orchestra. Reprising a job he had done in
the twenties, he was usually featured at the annual automobile
shows at the Hippodrome arena.[29]

The debut business was always big in the winter. Francis was
kept busy enough with debut dances for National Life heiresses.
Within forty-eight hours in 1938, his orchestra played for two of
them, Elizabeth Craig, granddaughter of founder C. A. Craig
and Cornelia Fort, daughter of founder Rufus Fort.[30]

Soon after his return to Nashville, Francis left the Andrew
Jackson Hotel and returned to the Hermitage Hotel. There
one could obtain lunch for sixty cents and dinner for one
dollar, both enhanced by Francis's music. The *couvert* charge
for a Saturday night dinner-dance was one dollar and fifty
cents.

He enlarged both his and the hotel's reputations when the
orchestra played for the second inaugural reception and ball of
Governor Hill McAlister on January 16, 1935. The hotel was
only two blocks from the Capitol; and its Union Street entrance
was just across the street from the swearing-in site, the War
Memorial Building. After a reception in the loggia that
evening, the ball was started by a grand march led by Governor
and Mrs. McAlister walking beneath an arch of sabers held by
National Guardsmen. The festivities may have been scaled back
because of the state's near empty Depression coffers.
Nevertheless, this was an honor for Francis; and reviewers
uniformly applauded the orchestra's work that night.[31]

In the 1930s, Craig latched onto a performance opportunity that was unheard of by later generations—playing in
movie theaters. In an era when moving pictures reigned
supreme, without television competition, in visual entertainment, customers could enjoy a full and varied slate of public
diversion—all for seventy-five cents, forty for youngsters. In
a residual vaudeville format, orchestras and feature acts
would entertain from the theater stage for as much as two
hours between screenings. Maintaining their characteristic
work ethic, Francis's group would hurry a block over from
the Hermitage Hotel after lunch and dinner to play their

shows, usually at the Loew's Church Street Theater. They shared billing with such hits as *The Stranger Returns* with Lionel Barrymore and Miriam Hopkins, *A Wicked Woman* with Mady Christians, and *Tugboat Annie* with Marie Dressler and Wallace Beery.

The most glamorous and locally important of these twin bills was the debut on November 27, 1935, at the Knickerbocker Theater of *Stars Over Broadway* with James Melton, "Nashville's Own Jimmy." In the six years since hitting New York, Craig's saxophonist and boy singer had become one of America's most popular radio tenors and launched a movie career. For several days before the debut, Melton held court from his suite at the Hermitage Hotel. He was welcomed by the governor and feted with a banquet. In addition to sharing the bill with Melton, Craig basked in the glow of the success of his friend and former employee.[32]

If all this activity were not enough, the band played engagements in numerous nightclubs during the thirties. There were occasional dates in Birmingham, Chattanooga, and Florida, but most were in Nashville. Among those spots were the Wagon Wheel on Harding Road (*couvert* charge usually seventy-five cents) and the Ridgeway Inn. In addition to Francis Craig's, the Wagon Wheel often featured other outstanding orchestras, including those of Tommy Dorsey, Bob Crosby, Vincent Lopez, Glen Gray, Clyde McCoy, and Ozzie Nelson. The Ridgeway Inn, which became the Club Embassy,

Advertisement for Stars Over Broadway, *featuring James Melton, and "his buddy," Francis Craig. (From the* Nashville Banner, *26 November 1935)*

Edwin Wilson (E. W.) Craig.
(Courtesy of Mrs. Walter Robinson)

was rougher. Better characterized as a roadhouse, illegal gambling was usually available there.[33]

The radio industry did well in the thirties. People were still buying sets. Between 1925 and 1940, U.S. households with radio sets increased ten-fold, from two million seven hundred fifty thousand to twenty-eight million five hundred thousand. WSM just kept being WSM, an aggressive, resourceful, successful radio station and National Life marketing tool. In preparation for increasing its power in 1932 to fifty thousand watts, the maximum allowable in the United States, it built what was then the tallest radio structure on the continent, an 878-foot tower out on Franklin Road. Its big wattage and clear channel designation assured its eminence in the mid-South. E. W. Craig continued his ascent through national broadcasting circles. In 1934, he became chairman of the Clear Channel Broadcasting Service. The station would solidify its national reputation in 1939 when the *Grand Ole Opry* became a regular Saturday night national broadcast on NBC.[34]

Prior to that milestone, however, Francis Craig had done his part to project Nashville's premier radio station onto the national scene. The orchestra did not have the time and apparently was not needed for as many local broadcasts as in the early days of WSM. Midday programs now catered to farmers, featuring market reports and country entertainment. In the early evening hours, the station now broadcast public service and news programs, soothing music from the hotels having apparently become passé.

Although more nationally known orchestras such as Tommy Dorsey's or Paul Whiteman's were heard in the prime evening hours, the Francis Craig Orchestra often broadcast fifteen or thirty minute segments over the network in the late hours, from 10:00 to 11:30 P.M. These were usually on Sundays but were occasionally on Monday or Tuesday. In addition to the quality Craig brought to the late-night national airways, big-city entertainment critics from the North were also impressed with the several major entertainers who had started with him. That such good music could come from the South was charming and surprising to Yankees.[35]

Both WSM and Francis took pride in these national distributions. Their principle value was marketing, as there was not much money from them. Still, Francis took them very seriously, polishing the product before sending it through the ether.

As in the 1920s, his relatives enjoyed the thrill of picking up his broadcasts from afar. His young cousin Corinne Howell (Dale), granddaughter of National Life founder E. B. Craig, heard Francis's orchestra aboard ship as she steamed toward Europe in the early 1930s.[36]

It is uncertain how much money was being made with all this work. The leader got most of the take from dance engagements. Throughout the thirties, his salaried players who worked at the Hermitage and WSM probably earned twenty-five to forty dollars per week. The nonunion vocalists got around twenty-five dollars per week. Work was somewhat seasonal, being more during debutante

Ridgeway Inn ad.

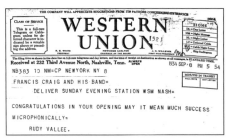

Congratulations telegram from Rudy Vallee.

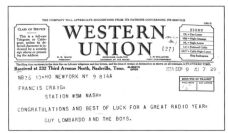

Congratulations telegram from Guy Lombardo.

and prom seasons and less in the summers, when musicians sometimes took off for resorts and fended for themselves.

Francis upped Clint Garvin to sixty-five dollars per week in 1935 in order to keep him from signing on with Bob Crosby. This seemed a point of pride to Francis, and Clint was never sure why he did it. It certainly made the other players mad. "The second sax was making more than the piano player." Musician income began to rise after 1940 due to the better economy and union pressure. [37]

One of the stories about Francis's reputed pecuniary tightness dealt with an accusation that he was not paying union scale in the late thirties. Several of his musicians were allegedly called before the union board. When Newt Richardson, one of his Alabama boys, was asked his name by the examining board, he blurted out the money amount that Francis had coached him to report as his income.[38] Well, maybe; but players were not bailing out from the band on account of their incomes, or lack thereof.

Along with a cadre of fine instrumentalists, Francis attracted plenty of marketable, occasionally talented feature "frontmen," many of whom would later make national splashes. There had been Jimmy Melton, Kenny Sargent, and Irene Beasley in the twenties. The stream of talented performers still flowed in the thirties. After his return from Denver in 1933, Craig's featured boy singer was Tommy Harrison, his trombonist. Alpha Louise Morton remained out front as girl singer for a couple of years, then moved on to Chicago, where she adopted the name Kay.

The Francis Craig Orchestra brought quality to the late-night national airways.

She was succeeded by Arleen Owens, who had formerly sung with her sisters in a trio with Red Nichols's band. In the mid-thirties, Francis hired a young tenor from Memphis, Snooky Landman (later Lanson), who would be one of his best vocalists, most frustrating employees, and best known graduates. Though she was associated more with WSM than Francis Craig, Dinah Shore also sang with his band; and Francis probably helped launch her career.[39]

ONE FOR THE OLD SCHOOL

F rancis Craig remained very devoted to Vanderbilt. There were obvious business reasons for being visible at and supportive of Nashville's premier university out on West End Avenue. His orchestra played more dances there by multiples than any other group. In his diary depiction of a late-thirties, libidinous, dance-crazy, pre-War Vanderbilt, Ben Austin had twenty-one references to Craig. Most referred to his performing on the campus, some to occasions at the Hermitage Hotel and Belle Meade Club.[40]

In a time when there was only one professional sports team in Nashville, the Nashville Vols baseball team, Vanderbilt was one of the principle social and journalistic focuses in town. Just as now, the interested public often gauged any school's value through its accomplishments in sports. In spite of its historic academic emphasis and the necessity to compete with academies not necessarily stressing that priority, Vanderbilt had fielded up to that time outstanding athletic teams. Football was always the bell-cow sport in the South. Up to 1937, Vanderbilt's football team had won 284 games while losing 93 and tying 26. Most of its success had been during the thirty-year career of the legendary coach Dan McGugin, who was succeeded by Ray Morrison in 1935. The team's success continued throughout the thirties. They beat both the traditional powerhouse Tennessee (UT) and Alabama teams in 1935 and came within a losing field goal (to Alabama) of going to the Rose Bowl in 1937.[41] Now that's not bad for a small, private school that a publicity tout successfully labeled "the Harvard of the South."

Francis rooted for the team as much as any real or sidewalk alumnus. Some of his favorite programs were Saturday pregame broadcasts from the Hermitage in which the band played fight songs, prognosticators predicted scores, and the WSM announcer excited listeners for the pending game broadcast.[42]

Francis showed his abiding loyalty in the best way he could, musically. On a Wednesday night before the Tennessee game on November 12, 1938, Francis wrote a fight song for Vandy. He premiered it on WSM two nights hence, and it was played at the game in Knoxville that Saturday. The students loved it and awarded it huzzahs before the traditional Thanksgiving game against Alabama at Tuscaloosa. (In those days, UT was not the final Vanderbilt opponent of the season.) Perhaps a harbinger of hard football times to come, Vanderbilt lost to UT and Bama, going scoreless in both games—but the song was great!

Initially entitled "When Vandy Starts to Fight," it was later called "Dynamite" and has rung across Vanderbilt's gyms and fields as its "official fight song" (as . stated on published sheet music) for over sixty years. The message of some lines was obscure, apparently depicting images of mythological or ancient battles. Still, the tune conveyed catchy, optimistic punch.

"Dynamite" sheet music cover.

DYNAMITE
Dynamite, dynamite,
When Vandy starts to fight,
Down the field with blood to yield,
If need be, save the shield,
If vict'ry's won, when battle's done
Then Vandy's name will rise in fame,
But, win or lose, The Fates will choose,
And Vandy's game will be the same,
Dynamite, Dynamite,
When Vandy starts to fight!

Francis was very pleased with it, never hesitating to claim pride of authorship. In later years, he sometimes questioned Vanderbilt's appreciation of the work and bridled at being unable to get free game tickets on account of it. Surely the Reverend Father Craig taught Francis that his reward would only come in heaven (Matt. 5:10).[43]

Craig wrote "Dynamite" the week before a Vanderbilt/Tennessee game in November 1938.

A PRIVATE AND PUZZLING MAN

B y the late 1930s, Francis Craig seemed to have dropped whatever thoughts he may have had during his younger, more vigorous years about a career on a bigger stage. Earlier on he had aspired to play the eastern colleges and hotels, where there was more reputation and possibly more money to be earned. The band had almost signed a contract with a big New York hotel in 1934, but arrangements fell through at the last moment. Now, in addition to a cornucopia of local business, he had a respectable national reputation through his orchestra's repetitive airing over NBC. The network liked his neat, restful, sweet music in the late Sunday night hours; but neither New York nor Hollywood music moguls were seriously ringing his telephone. Well, who needed that bother?

Craig was quite busy in Nashville and environs. If ego were a consideration, he had plenty of southern fame. Country music was beginning to crowd live pop groups off the WSM programs, but Francis's orchestra had been one of the station's premier performers and still got publicity and a little money for the occasional evening slot on cousin E. W.'s station.

His association with the Hermitage Hotel was secure and pleasing to all parties. Francis enjoyed the demure, convivial work; the hotel advertised on billboards his availability at the Hermitage Grill. The musicians could almost sleepwalk through the easy music. Over time, Francis had successfully gotten them to play *piano* enough not to interfere with conversations. A meal at the Hermitage was an occasion, not just purchased nourishment. Diners dressed formally, in sync with the décor, food, and entertainment. Marjorie Arnold, daughter of the Vanderbilt Law School dean and a Vandy coed, remembered with bliss luncheon dates at the Hermitage with her suitor, Edward Kirby, who was in charge of WSM's marketing. Though they did not attribute their subsequent marriage to Craig's soft strains and conversation over a red rose, neither felt the ambience hurt their romance either.[44]

Francis was most comfortable in this milieu, thriving on being a mannerly host and often personalizing the music.

Hermitage billboard advertising the Francis Craig Orchestra.

Midshipman Doris Kelly could pick up his broadcasts at the Naval Academy. When Kelly went to lunch at the Hermitage while on vacation, the orchestra broke into "Anchors Aweigh" when he entered the room. D. Y. Proctor came down to lunch from his honeymoon night at the hotel and was greeted with the wedding march. The Grill Room was Craig's parlor, and polite guests were warmly welcomed.[45]

Dances played by Francis Craig were featured almost every Saturday night at the Belle Meade Country Club, of which Edwin Craig was president from 1930–1932. Then there were the jitter-buggers out at Vanderbilt and every Greek fraternal organization east of the Mississippi and south of the Ohio Rivers. In addition to his college jobs, hardly a winter weekend passed without his playing for one of the several Nashville high school fraternities. In an era when teenagers found other ways than wearing bizarre clothing to separate themselves from their elders, young Nashvillians enjoyed dressing formally for the orchestra's dances. There was a reassuring routine to these affairs, beginning with the Grand March and including dance cards of "no-breaks." Francis was a great model of decorum and good taste on the bandstand, pleasing to both dancers and their parents.

Of course there were the more organic pleasures to be derived from such an evening. One formerly young buck recalled the terrific privilege of holding close all the sweet-smelling girls during the last no-break, for which Craig usually played "Beloved." Just as delightful, then and in retrospect, was his traditional closing number, "When Day Is Done." Francis Craig's was indisputably the best dance orchestra in town.[46]

The Francis Craigs were not really rolling in dough but were well enough off, especially by Depression standards. Reflecting his bountiful business, Francis was secure enough to finance an upgrade in lifestyle.

Horace G. Hill, a regional grocery magnate and real estate investor, decided to domestically develop his big farm on the western outskirts of Nashville. The development of Hillwood Estates had been delayed by the Depression. In addition to the Hill and Wentworth Caldwell (Mr. Hill's son-in-law) compounds, there was only one other residence on the property by the late thirties. Craig's friend, Ferris Bailey, had built that home. As Hill felt some urgency about getting the project underway, Bailey urged Craig to buy the lot adjacent to his and come to the suburbs with him.

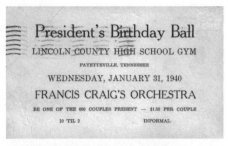

President's Birthday Ball
LINCOLN COUNTY HIGH SCHOOL GYM
FAYETTEVILLE, TENNESSEE
WEDNESDAY, JANUARY 31, 1940
FRANCIS CRAIG'S ORCHESTRA
BE ONE OF THE 600 COUPLES PRESENT — $1.50 PER COUPLE
10 TIL 2   INFORMAL

Another high school gig. (Postcard courtesy of Ridley Wills II)

Craig hesitated so much about making the move that one day in summer 1936, Bailey just informed Francis that he had bought two lots next to his for $2,600. Once more a caring friend had forcefully guided him well. Another would build his house. Fraternity brother Ed Keeble, now a prominent and successful architect, designed their house on 202 Hillwood Drive (the Baileys were at 200). The two-story, brick, West Indies-style residence atop a spacious lot featured a cantilevered balcony above the front porch and access to balconies from all upstairs bedrooms. Ferris's wife, Clara, helped decorate the house, finished in 1938. It cost $35,000 to build, a tidy sum considering that the average cost of a new house in the United States that year was $3,900. Though perhaps just below the mansion category, Francis had at least a big, stylish house. It was to be the Craigs' home for almost thirty years.[47]

As he approached the two-score mark in age, Francis seemed a content man. His income was good, his station secure, and his family healthy. Aside from Elizabeth and the girls, his time-consuming work seemed Francis's only interest. He continued to occasionally compose. He was not a reader and rarely seemed to have studied opinions on matters of current

The Craigs' home. (Courtesy of Elizabeth Lancaster)

economic or political interest. Other than some occasional walks around Hillwood, he had no athletic interests—not golf, tennis, or outdoor sports.

Even private times were dominated by Craig's work. The Craig household had to be absolutely quiet the mornings after his late nights so that the maestro could get his sleep. This prohibition on noisemaking extended to guests and neighborhood kids. Everyone knew when Mr. Craig had worked the night before. Francis expected and appreciated such deferences. Elizabeth saw that he got them.

Craig's friends and family were constantly trying to steer him into *some* hobby. After the move to the spacious, then rural Hillwood property, Elizabeth and Ferris Bailey suggested a chicken-raising project for him. After a requisite period of resistance, Francis built a fine, modern coop—which lay unoccupied for months. In frustration, the persistent Bailey stocked the house one day while Francis was at work.

Proponents of the poultry project had foreseen it as a potentially wonderful experience in animal husbandry for the Craig girls. Wrong! Though gathering eggs was fun, alleged allergies kept the city-girl teenagers from pursuing the more dirty, malodorous, character-building chores. Francis, a man seemingly sans enthusiasms, looked upon the whole operation with benign neglect. So, his austere and polished wife paid the price for trying to fill her husband's leisure hours and took care of the birds. Within a couple of years, most all the New Hampshire Red and White Rock chickens had graced the Craig board. The maid, Fanny, not Elizabeth, had wrung their necks. One could only go so far. Francis's loved ones had finally learned that his hobby was his work.[48]

Such anecdotes suggest that Craig was apparently an uncomplicated, enigmatic, man. As one observer noted, "He was a character and didn't even know it."

Impressions of him varied radically, depending on perspective. His audiences probably saw him as he wanted them to. While delivering an outstanding product, he was handsome, cordial, and neatly turned out. He was closemouthed and rarely spoke in public. When he did, people heard a soft, delicious southern drawl more suggestive of the nineteenth century than the twentieth. His movements were economical and graceful. He exuded savoir faire.

There were diverse opinions about him even by people in the entertainment business. Band musicians were notoriously fun loving, and Craig had absolutely no bonhomie with them. His quiet demeanor and lack of closeness to his employees caused one player to say he was "already dead." Another called him a puritan.

Perhaps he kept a stiff distance from his players in order to maintain his executive authority. He ran his band well and was respected for being "all business." He maintained excellent discipline without ever raising his voice or seeming to get mad. The younger players called him the "great white father." Despite grumbling about the squareness of his music, especially in his latter years, most musicians thought he had a good band for its purpose.

Francis was universally polite to and protective of women, including his employees. Mary Cortner (Ragland) occasionally sang with the orchestra in the early thirties at the Hermitage and WSM. She called him a "lovely" gentleman, despite his having cancelled a date she had with the orchestra's violinist. There would be no romantic entanglements at his office.

Only occasionally would he allow a glimpse of a thoroughly repressed sense of humor. One player remembered the prudish Francis quietly joking about splashing on some aftershave as he returned from a late-night job to the marital boudoir. When a trumpeter, Bill McDowell, surreptitiously nipped too much from his flask during a job and was feeling the worse for wear, he made the mistake of riding back to Nashville with Craig. The abstemious leader in his most Methodist manner quietly but repetitively intoned, " . . . but the way of transgressors is hard" (Prov. 13:15), until the inebriated one screamed, "Just shut up, Francis." Aside from the poor fellow's disrespect, the boss probably fired him because he had

Elizabeth with Donia and Celeste. (From the Birmingham News-Age-Herald, *2 February 1937)*

been drinking, something Craig would not tolerate.

His vocabulary was equally chaste. Craig's idea of a dirty joke would have probably been acceptable at a Methodist camp meeting. A real knee-slapper was the answer to the query, "How do you make holy water?" "Why, you just boil the hell out of it!" The closest thing to an expletive that passed Francis's lips was the quaint "My Scots," his all-purpose expression of incredulity.[49]

A peculiar dynamic of Craig's relationship with his employees was the penchant of the boys to play jokes on him—a proclivity of his best friends as well. They seemed to go to the point of disrespect without violating it. Most of the jokes were harmless but had a consistent theme; Francis was the butt, not the perpetrator of the jokes. The stories are legion and have doubtless grown over the years. They had a million of 'em.

When the blind Bob Lamm was with the band in the mid-forties, band members played a transportation trick involving his disability. On the way back from a dance in Huntsville, Alabama, Francis looked up from his car to see one of their convoy passing his. It was being "driven" by Bob Lamm! Of course someone was stooped beside him actually steering the auto. Another variant of the same trick was to plant the three-foot, nine-inch tall Pee Wee Marquette in the driver's seat and speed by the boss's car.

Francis was very proud of his long affiliation with NBC. He was particularly conscientious about his Sunday night network program. On an April first, the gang set the studio clocks ahead a few minutes. At the scheduled hour for the program, Craig lowered the beat and began to experience a musical disaster. The trumpet player fell off a note. The drummer knocked over his trap set. Horns were out of tune. Before the true time for the program and before Francis had a stroke, they let him in on the joke.

Near the end of his career, Francis employed a small electronic keyboard at which he would doodle intros or themes. For some reason, his traditional musicians resented this device. They found numerous ways of frustrating his use of it. Trumpeter Mickey Tennity sitting in the back might suddenly unplug it while Francis was in the midst of a solo. Once someone (probably John Gordy) inserted a device into the machine similar to a Christmas tree light flasher that interrupted juice to it. Francis was as frustrated with the music shop's inevitable inability to find anything wrong with the keyboard as he was the periodic loss of sound from it.

Some of the tension between the bandleader and his band doubtless sprang from his careful use of money, for which he became, correctly or not, infamous. Again, the anecdotes are numerous and probably at least partially apocryphal. There were enough of them to also suggest they might convey the truth. He supposedly was discomfited by the necessity to pay hotel bills and ("My Scots!") resented anyone buying a steak while on the road. A trombone player who substituted for a Sunday afternoon at the Hermitage Hotel was paid pro rata for his time and left with a check for $2.79. After a wartime Coca-Cola Spotlight Band Show, he publicly awarded the band a choice bottle of Scotch whiskey for their fine performance, only to later request it back. When Francis gave his regulars Stetson hats one Christmas, he gave a part-time bassist a tie. The man was not a spendthrift.

Francis was introverted and not especially charming to anyone in whom he had no interest. In addition to being generally quiet, he was also characterized as aloof, egotistical, snobbish, prissy, vague, and an old maid. Confusion about his family origin and (alleged) wealth colored the perceptions of many, who thought he was a rich man, one of the insurance Craigs. Francis may have felt himself in a social no-man's land. He played at the Belle Meade Club; he was not a member of it. No matter his success, his career was in the entertainment business, not one historically pursued by respectable people or the elite, among whom his cousins were now leaders. He made his living by showing up for work every day but rejected the loose, colorful mannerisms of his fellow musicians and studiously enveloped himself in an aristocratic patina.[50]

To close friends and family, however, Craig was warm, tolerant, kind, gentle, gracious, and (always) polite. In contrast to some outsiders who considered him too big for his britches, those close to him thought him honestly humble. The most comprehensive characterization by those who loved him was that he was "sweet." It is unclear why he did not share these personal features with others outside his circle.

A miasma of detachment or vagueness seemed to interfere with his relationship to the rest of the world. Some said this was part of his artistic temperament and that his mind was simply on his music. Others said he just didn't get things. A very literate acquaintance compared him to Owen Garrett in Henry James's *The Spoils of Poynton*, a good man with moral sensibility, who was delightfully dense and relied on the attentive love of others. Whatever the accuracy of that, Francis always had the love of devoted friends and a strong, smart wife, who was obviously the more personable and extroverted of the couple.

When he had time for it, Craig's favorite socializing was at small dinner parties with friends, at which a capability as a quiet raconteur made him comfortable and attractive. An admirer called him *très simple*, meaning without pretense. His lifestyle was neither affected nor extravagant, and there was no indication he would ever want or be able to do otherwise. His was a life of contrasts, a private man in a public job. None who knew him well believed him anything other than a simple, good person, who was blessedly and successfully pursuing his calling as a bandleader.

No, he was not *going* anywhere. He had already *come* from the bedroom of a Dickson, Tennessee, parsonage to a plush home in Nashville; from overt poverty to financial security; from leading a musical combo at a college fraternity dance to leading "The South's Most Popular Orchestra." If his avowed preference for life at home (i.e., Nashville) and the security of his situation were not reasons enough to abjure seeking success in a bigger pond, he did not now have the ambition or energy to do so. Though he remained trim and attractive, candid pictures of the time show Francis looking somewhat older than usual for his age. A lifetime of working long hours, a chronic lack of exercise, and too many Chesterfields were taking their toll on him. As he advanced into the middle years, there was every reason to believe he would wind down and ride off into the musical sunset. Whatever such plans he might have had were to be interrupted by international events.

WORLD WAR II

L ike the rest of the nation, Tennessee in 1940 seemed to be slowly emerging from the Depression. The Tennessee Valley Authority (TVA), one of President Franklin Roosevelt's pet federal public works projects, apparently bode well for the state, promising available and cheap electricity and flood control. Tennessee was still a relatively poor state. Per capita income was only $360, *down* 4 percent from a decade earlier.

Nashville's population was now 167,402. Though Davidson County had grown somewhat faster, the city's population had only increased 9 percent since 1930. There were signs, though, that big times lay ahead for Nashville, even though potential prosperity might be caused by war.

It was unclear that the United States would enter any war. After Hitler's invasion of Poland in 1939, a martial lull in Europe, the so-called "phony war," set in. The time for negotiations seemed ripe. Led by the America First movement, there was considerable opposition to U.S. involvement in yet another of Europe's wars. Then there was the 1940 campaign pledge of Roosevelt's to avoid any such horror. Interventionists and isolationists fiercely debated the appropriate U.S. role. The cast of the nation's international die became more obvious throughout 1941. Any doubts about Roosevelt's strategic inclinations were erased by the institution of the military draft and the Lend Lease Act, which essentially provided free war materiel for Great Britain and her allies.

Nashville's prominent role in rearmament was epitomized by the opening of the Vultee Aircraft plant in May 1941. City leaders took huge pride in the plant, which would employ seven thousand workers to manufacture bombers. Various other new and established manufacturers modified their lines to make products for the booming war market. City leaders saw Nashville as an "inner citadel" during any potential conflict. That conflict arrived on December 7, 1941, with the Japanese attack on Pearl Harbor. The citizens of the Volunteer State and its capital were ready to serve. The Tennessee Depression ended precipitously with the onset of war. In the U.S., the state ranked twenty-first in value of military facilities built, sixteenth in nonwar-related manufacturing facilities built, and thirteenth in publicly financed industrial and manufacturing facilities built during the War.[51]

Nashville became a military crossroads. Several military bases sprung up in Middle Tennessee—Camp Forrest in Tullahoma, Camp Campbell near Clarksville, Smyrna Air Field. For topographical and climactic reasons, Middle Tennessee was ideal for military training. All these boys had to go somewhere when on leave, and that usually was Nashville. It was estimated that over one million soldiers visited the city during the War's first year, taxing the city's hospitality facilities. Inevitable wartime problems of venereal disease and juvenile delinquency also strained Nashville's public health and social fabric.[52]

There was little chance Francis Craig would be called, but he dutifully registered for the draft. He had long lost the corpulence packed onto his five feet, ten and one-half inch frame at the Oakes Home and in 1942 weighed in as a middleweight at 165 pounds.[53] Uncle Sam did not want him on the lines but would take advantage of his services on the home front. He would as usual have plenty to do.

It is unlikely many enlisted men could afford the Hermitage Hotel, but their officers and transient government officials had to stay somewhere. The hotel was full and could still afford a house orchestra, an economic fact well appreciated by the Craigs. Francis rarely corresponded, but he wrote to Howard Baughman in 1944 to effusively thank him for the continuing opportunity. "Wherever I go—Whatever I do—I shall never forget how kind you have been to me throughout these years." This was in response to a clipping forwarded by Baughman that congratulated Francis for his record of twenty-one consecutive years at the Hermitage, " . . . a world's record for one band in one spot."[54] No one knows who tabulated this truly indoor record.

There was much less traveling for the orchestra during the War due to gasoline rationing and decreased formal entertaining. It was unseemly and impossible to continue the usual social routines with most of the boys mustered into the service, many at mortal risk. There were still local opportunities for dance work. Belle Meade Country Club did not require a road trip, being less than three miles from Francis's home. The club's 1941 New Year's Eve dinner dance was broadcast nationally over NBC. Life goes on.

WSM was busy and expansive. In 1941, WSM-FM became the first licensed frequency modulation (FM) station in the nation. Management claimed that the Air Castle produced more NBC-AM (amplitude modulation) network programs than any station in the U.S. outside New York, Los Angeles, or Chicago. After 1943, NBC carried coast-to-coast a thirty minute segment of the *Opry*, sponsored by Prince Albert tobacco. Among the ways WSM nurtured the troops flooding the area was a one-hour Sunday afternoon program called "The National Life Canteen," which featured all their entertainers, including Francis Craig. Half the program was broadcast; the other half was a studio party with entertainment and refreshments.

WSM's big war boost was unquestionably the increased popularity of country music. The Camel Caravan sponsored tours of *Opry* stars to military bases at home and abroad. Many "city" soldiers had had no exposure to hillbilly music and came to appreciate it as much as their country cousins. In broadcasting retorts to invading Americans on Okinawa, the Japanese said "To hell with President Roosevelt! To hell with Babe Ruth! To hell with *Roy Acuff!*" (emphasis added)! WSM (and Roy Acuff) in coming decades would cash a huge dividend on all this wartime dissemination of country music.[55]

Francis's association with WSM seemed more prominent than ever during the War. The station called him its music director, but the honor or responsibility of that designation was uncertain. They also assigned the title to Pietro Brescia and Beasley Smith, who directed the station orchestra. Francis's thirty-minute late Sunday night national broadcast, now called *Francis Craig's Sunday Night Serenade*, was a regular thing through 1945.

Then there was the added work of entertaining troops.
Dolly Dearman (Denny) was a dancer who had worked with
Francis at some of his Loew's Theater shows in the thirties.
Now he called on her to help entertain the troops at regional
military bases. She recalled taking these trips "almost every
Sunday afternoon." Both she and Anne Vaughn (Parman), a
Vandy coed who sang with the band, appreciated his solicitous
attention to them. When the band returned from such
concerts, he always drove them home or followed them to be
sure they arrived safely—ever the gentleman. Francis's services
were also featured twice on prestigious "Spotlight Band"
national broadcasts from military bases.[56]

In unquestionably doing his part for the war effort, Francis
sometimes had to scramble for personnel. Trombonists, for
instance, kept getting drafted out from under him. Though many
of his wartime players would later contribute to the Nashville
music business (e.g., pianist John Gordy), Francis did not have
the consistent flow of outstanding talent he had previously
enjoyed. Kitty Kallen was a conspicuous exception. For a brief
time, Francis had one of the best combinations of boy and girl
singers imaginable, Kitty Kallen and Snooky Landman (Lanson).

If matters were not complicated enough for musicians, there
were union and organizational struggles that would fundamen-
tally affect the band business contemporaneously and after the
War. Though record sales in 1941 had been the best since 1921,
problems loomed for that business. Manufacturers were already
struggling with the wartime rationing of shellac and Vinylite
needed to surface the disks. Then the industry was hit with a
strike. The boycott of the recording industry by the American
Federation of Musicians (AFM) had no immediate effect on
Francis but was one of the factors that would cause a seemingly
premature end to the Big Band era within a decade.

James Caesar Petrillo was president of the AFM. His union
was in agreement with record companies on at least one matter.
The companies, musicians, and bandleaders all worried about the
looming threat of recorded music formats on radio. The companies (incorrectly) felt that the opportunity to repeatedly hear a
single disk bought by a station would discourage retail sales. The

musicians foresaw the end of live broadcasting, an economic necessity that had already occurred in smaller stations. Petrillo intended to protect his members. A comprehensive boycott of the recording industry began in summer 1942. Settlement occurred with Decca in early 1943, but not with the other major players, Columbia and RCA-Victor, until 1944. The companies agreed after arbitration to pay a tax into the union's benefit fund.

Though Petrillo could crow about victory, it was a Pyrrhic one. The companies had not suffered, and a basic change in radio broadcasting, detrimental to the strikers' original goals, had occurred. The companies had made plenty of money recording for the federal government, and the practice of spinning records over the airways was more prevalent than before. A careful observer even might have foreseen the end of live radio entertainment. Another result was that during the strike singers could record with vocal backgrounds. This was the first step of their eventual emergence over bands in the public favor. There is no indication that Francis Craig recognized that several termites were nibbling at the foundation of his professional house.[57]

More immediately obvious effects on Craig's career and the music industry in Nashville were created by the struggle between performance-rights societies. The American Society of Composers, Authors and Publishers (ASCAP) had, since its inception in 1914, become a powerful advocate, providing regular performance compensation from licensees (radio stations, theaters, movie companies, etc.) for its members' works. The organization was so successful that it limited its perspective and overestimated its necessity.

Its principal opposition was the National Association of Broadcasters (NAB), which had objected to ASCAP's charging broadcasters since 1932 a percentage of radio advertising sales for use of their members' products. NAB asserted this practice was monopolistic, and ASCAP found itself in continual legislative and judicial struggles throughout the thirties. As the deadline for licensee contract renewals approached in 1940, ASCAP flagrantly stalled negotiations. The power play did not work. In October 1939, NAB formed Broadcast Music, Incorporated (BMI), a competitive performing rights organization. In late

1940, ASCAP demanded an exorbitant seven and one-half percent of gross sales from the broadcasters and threatened a prohibition on the use of its music. NAB called their bluff and told them to take a walk. On January 1, 1941, the great ASCAP ban of its music from radio went into place.

During the job action, those members heard on radio had to use non-ASCAP themes. Craig temporarily put his beloved "Red Rose" back in the catalog and used a forgettable, old public domain number called "Disallusioned" *(sic)*, an appropriate description for what ASCAP members would retrospectively feel about their strike. ASCAP caved and accepted a two and three-quarters-percent licensee payment on December 31, 1941.

The ban was a failure for ASCAP and a triumph for BMI and the listening public, who benefited from new competition. ASCAP had always favored publishers of music from Broadway and Hollywood, to the detriment of those producing other forms such as folk, country-western, gospel, and Latin music. Now those artists had a year of uncluttered airways to strut their professional stuff, and the public loved it. Additionally, BMI offered a new, simpler payment method. Remuneration came through the publisher to writers for units played on air. BMI welcomed country writers, who were beginning to congregate in Nashville. The more egalitarian organization was later also more hospitable to rock musicians.

Edwin Craig was instrumental in the broadcasters' tough stand and the organization of BMI. As a board member, he led the reorganization of NAB in the late thirties. His ground-breaking work in helping establish an alternative to ASCAP was recognized at BMI's 1965 annual dinner in New York when the organization gave him a special award. This effort had little effect on the career of his ASCAP-loyal cousin, Francis; but it was a huge contribution to country music and Nashville, which postwar would become Music City.[58]

ANTICLIMAX

As World War II ended in August 1945, Craig's career began to decline for reasons esthetic, economic, and personal. He probably did not immediately recognize this drift. Returning vets enjoyed musically enhanced dinners at the Hermitage as much as their sweethearts and wives had during their absence. Nashville's swells still danced at the Belle Meade Club and other comfortable venues. Francis had simply outlasted competitors such as Red McEwen (a former trumpeter in Francis's band) and Jimmy Gallagher (a former saxist in the band), but Owen Bradley's new potent orchestra was now available to buyers. On late Sunday nights, the *Francis Craig Serenade* still aired, hosted by WSM announcers familiar to postwar audiences—Jud Collins, Ott Devine, Ernie Keller, and Irving Waugh. When Craig played at Cherry Point (North Carolina) Naval Station, he was called "one of the greatest names in music in the South." His reputation was solid, but such things are ephemeral and based on fickle public taste.[59]

Adventurous, talented musicians inevitably experimented with new forms during the War years. In avant-garde clubs, brilliant soloists backed by small combos pushed the musical envelope through the artistic and semantical categories of bebop to bop to "progressive jazz." Among these innovators were John Coltrane, Thelonious Monk, Charlie Parker, and Lester Young. Soon after the War, bands such as those of Woody Herman and Stan Kenton had incorporated their styles. Though evolutionary, the music was rhythmically unpredictable, often melodiously confusing, and almost impossible to dance to. Critical musicologists did not consider that feature part of the definition of valuable jazz and concluded the new music was better. Where had swing gone?

Lots of social changes had occurred in World War II that would require adjustments by everyone. Now in his mid-forties, Francis Craig seemed set-in-his-ways to the point of rigidity. He was not growing younger by watching or learning from youth. Rather, he seemed so comfortable in his tastes and work that he might have lost the opportunism that characterized his salad days. The volatile and candid Kitty Kallen had characterized his frame of mind when she told him that he was as "dated as the knot on your tie."[60]

The postwar Francis Craig was a middle-aged, musical troglodyte. Though he might have been considered a hepcat in the twenties and was a marginal swinger in the thirties,

Craig's orchestra flies to Cherry Point Naval Station, 1946. WSM announcer Jud Collins is on left, Craig is third from left.

he certainly was not a cool cat in the forties.[61] Even the WSM studio musicians called his music "ticky-tack." Numerous Craig players over the years had complained of the boredom of playing his music. Many analogized the orchestra to Guy Lombardo's, saying Craig wanted to be a Southern Guy Lombardo. If Francis ever recognized this criticism, like Lombardo he probably had cried over the artistic denigration—all the way to the bank.

Though he might please his dancing customers with something as wild as "Beat Me Daddy Eight to the Bar," he bridled at the new "whang diddy whang whang of jive." He liked music one could sing and remember. "It's my orchestra—we'll play what I like." Considering the audiences he served, this was an apparently reasonable attitude. It might also have indicated his time was past.

Another radical change on bandstands was the new emphasis on vocalists to the detriment of the orchestra. This resulted from labor strife and changes in listener psyche.

During the almost two years of the disastrous recording strike, the best bands could not bring new work to their fans. Nonunion singers, often backed by *a capella* courses, could. A reflective and worried public began to prefer the tender notes of Frank Sinatra, Peggy Lee, Dick Haymes, Dinah Shore, and Nat Cole to the urgent arrangements of big bands. The first huge vocal hit was "Paper Doll," by the Mills Brothers in 1943. The top recording artists for the period 1940–1955 included only three bands; the others were singers. No longer would natty, curly boy or gorgeous, sequined girl singers sit patiently at the side of the stage, flashing their pearly whites while waiting for a single course in a long number. No, they would be featured, perhaps backed by their former employers or a smaller, less expensive combo. "But many that are first shall be last; and the last shall be first" (Matt. 19:30).

The Big Band era was over. There would be numerous resuscitations of those terrific bands and their timeless music. However, the demise of their preeminence could almost be pinpointed to December 1946, when within a few weeks the orchestras of Les Brown, Benny Carter, Tommy Dorsey, Benny Goodman, Woody Herman, Ina Ray Hutton, Harry James, and Jack Teagarden temporarily or permanently disbanded.[62]

Things were also changing in radio. Since their advent, the stronger stations had resembled theater companies, with their own musicians, actors, and special effects. During the thirties, Dinah Shore was the most outstanding example of WSM's numerous talented staff who would have important careers beyond the South. Christine Johnson (Smith) had come to Nashville from Owensboro, Kentucky, to study at the Nashville Conservatory of Music under Sr. de Luca. She worked at WSM to make ends meet, starring in such musical shows as *Magnolia Blossoms*. She won a Metropolitan Opera audition in 1943 but ended up on Broadway, where she premiered the role of Aunt Nellie Fowler in *Carousel*.

Bobby Tucker, considered the best popular pianist in Nashville, later enjoyed a successful career in music arrangement on Broadway and in Hollywood. Madge West was the dramatics instructor at the station before moving to New York for a career of radio drama and television advertising. The singer Johnny Payne went from WSM to New York and was featured for many years at the Monkey Bar. Dick Dudley, a Father Ryan and Vanderbilt educated Nashvillian, went from WSM announcing and drama to become a well-recognized announcer for the big NBC outlets in New York. Marj Cooney came from Huntsville, Alabama, to play studio piano for almost twenty years at WSM. She left the station in 1950 to work for one of the biggest national talent agencies, Columbia Artist's Management Association. Ed Kirby was in charge of the station's public relations through much of the 1930s. He supposedly coined the phrase "Air Castle of the South," by which WSM became widely known. Before World War II, he became the first public relations director for the National Association of Broadcasters. During the war, as Colonel Kirby, he was chief of the Radio Branch of the War Department, Bureau of Public Relations. At war's end, he became director of public relations for the USO.[63]

WSM long prided itself on such a staff and had almost no record library except sound effects until the late 1940s. The FCC and the musician's union had always looked askance on nonlive entertainment. Additionally, recording stars often refused to have their records played because of exclusive network contracts.

However, recurrent court struggles resulted by 1940 in broadcasters being able to buy and play records without restraint. A new airway hero, the disk jockey (DJ), would now emerge. Many smaller spots on the dial, so called *coffee pots,* had stayed afloat for years by the inexpensive technique of having someone spin platters while furiously shilling for the station and their sponsors. The technique acquired some class and legitimacy through the wartime "Make Believe Ballroom" programs of Martin Block in New York and Al Jarvis in Hollywood. Now postwar "personalities" such as Arthur Godfrey, Steve Allen, and Tennessee Ernie Ford could achieve fame and wealth on entertaining programs that, incidentally, were less expensive to produce. How much longer did even wealthy WSM need Francis Craig's services if it already had a studio orchestra under Beasley Smith?[64]

Hotel economics must have changed as well. The Hermitage had long proudly touted Francis's years of "continual" service at the hotel. Those touting that fluctuating number, always in excess of two decades, seemed to disregard his year away for TB therapy, his tours (one of which lasted almost a year), and his fleeting infidelity with the Andrew Jackson Hotel. The bottom line usually prevails over sentimentality though. Bands were now too expensive for most hotels. Hermitage management did not renew Francis's contract after 1947. The most secure brace in his financial foundation had been removed.

All these economic disruptions seemed to have little effect on the stoical band man. Any disappointment or anger he might have felt was blunted by fatigue. Craig was flat-out tired—tired of dealing with musicians, tired of travelling, tired of the vagaries of the music business. His lack of energy to fight the battle of life seems to have coincided with his professional obsolescence. He decided to retire. Before his final NBC broadcast on May 4, 1947, Francis received a congratulatory telegram from the Vanderbilt Phis, "May your future be as successful as your past."[65] With little ado, he disbanded the Francis Craig Orchestra.

The frugal Francis probably had a nice nest egg, but he was still young enough to appreciate a little cash flow. Once more, family connections helped. WSM allegedly hired him to be one of the new titans of the airways, a disk jockey. Why not? If WSM, through the Craigs, had been good for Francis, he had also been mighty good for WSM. On reassessment, the hirer quickly recognized that Francis may not have had the ideal personality to be a competitive DJ and promptly changed the job description to record librarian—good choice!

As Francis Craig (apparently) rode out to pasture, he could recall pridefully an excellent career. In doing what he loved most, leading a dance orchestra, he had achieved a big, reputable southern reputation and a modest national one. In Nashville, his band for over twenty years had been the best and the one needed for really important occasions. All the while, he had well cared for his family and comported himself as a true Southern Gentleman. He had worked very hard and deserved a rest. "Well done, thou good and faithful servant . . . " (Matt. 25:21).

CHAPTER FOUR

There's just   one   place for   me,   NEAR YOU.

allegro ma non troppo

A Fast Tempo, but Not Too Much

Due to a peculiar combination of Francis Craig's honed talent, a considerate gesture for his family, and unfathomable public taste, his career in 1947 was to rise from the ashes of "semi-retirement" to unexpected fame and fortune. He was to disprove Leo Durocher's assertion that nice guys finish last. In the artistic equivalent of winning the World Series with a homer in the bottom of the ninth inning of the seventh game or, locally, beating the University of Tennessee in football with a last minute one-hundred-yard run, he would surprise his town, his family, and himself. Francis Craig would become what every obscure working stiff only fantasizes being, Number One.

"NEAR YOU"—A MUSICAL PHENOMENON

Nashville's first real recording session had been in September and October of 1928. A mobile crew of the Victor Talking Machine Company stopped in Nashville on the way back home to Atlanta from Memphis, both of which were significant early recording centers. In seven days, they recorded ten country acts, including The Binkley Brothers, an Opry hoedown band, and Warmack's Gully Jumpers. Sixty-nine songs were recorded at the Young Men's Christian

Association building. Thirty-six were released. None was a big seller. Nothing of any commercial note had occurred since.

After World War II, it was clear to most observers that Nashville was now a commercial music center for many reasons, most relating to country music. BMI's emergence had given country musicians a reliable, remunerative outlet for their products. The *Opry* was rising in national popularity. Performers and writers were beginning to congregate in the town. Acuff-Rose Publishing, the first of many important Nashville music publication houses, was founded in 1942.

Established stars still had to travel to Chicago, Cincinnati, or New York to get recorded. Why not have that capability in Nashville where the performers and writers were? Among those most wanting that capability in Nashville were a new group of recording professionals, the A & R (artists and repertoire) men. These record company executives were responsible for recognizing a good song, matching it with musicians, choosing a recording studio, and overseeing the session—in other words producing the records.

Some of the first to recognize this vacuum in Nashville and seek solutions for it were several employees of WSM. Carl Jenkins, George Reynolds, and Aaron Shelton were engineers at the station. Reynolds had helped Jack DeWitt put the station together in 1925. Shelton's career with the station tracked that of DeWitt's. Affectionately know as "A" at WSM, he was a radio-phile who in 1928 left Vanderbilt before graduating to work for the Air Castle of the South. He had some recording experience, having done some transcriptions for Armour Fertilizer at WSM in 1939. The station continued that business into the mid-1940s for companies such as Black Draught and Purina, using proven performers such as Eddy Arnold and Jamup and Honey.[1]

The engineers had no money, but they did have expertise and the favor of WSM. Financed with a thousand-dollar loan from Third National Bank, they bought some used recording equipment and persuaded the station to let them lease some space in one of its four studios. Flagrantly plagiarizing their famous employer's tag, they called their company the *Castle* Recording Laboratory.

Jim Bulleit was a thirtyish Indianan who had knocked around the management end of the entertainment business since college. Failure had dogged his career, but he had the irrepressible optimism of a natural entrepreneur. "If I looked at my mistakes, I wouldn't do anything. I just go on ahead." He was in 1946 the manager of WSM's Artist Service Bureau, a booking service for station talent.

With the encouragement of gospel recording star Wally Fowler, Bulleit decided to start an independent record company. With one thousand dollars from a mortgage on his house, he and partners J. V. Hitchcock and Fowler founded Bullet Recording and Transcription Company in April 1946. Fowler suggested the play on Bulleit's name for the company. Their first recording was "Zeb's Mountain Boogie," by the firm's music director, the increasingly visible Owen Bradley. Bulleit intended to mainly record *Opry* talent but soon branched into "race" and gospel music. Leaving no musical stone unturned, Bulleit became interested in filling a void in the company's repertoire by getting into popular music. Enter Francis Craig.

Francis was either nostalgic or restless and could not completely break away from making music. Though he had none yet, grandchildren were on his mind. He decided as a postlude to his career to make a record for his children's children, something about which they might say, "Yep, that's Grandpap—Pretty corny, but it was all him, that number." That record would give his grandchildren more to remember than he could have dreamed possible.

Lillian Dobson (Dunnavant), a pal of Craig's daughter Donia, claimed to have heard at its inception the tune that would catapult Craig's fame far from Nashville. During a 1946 weekend visit to the Craigs, "Mr. Francis" called the girls into the living room early one morning and played a tune he had been working on the preceding night. The girls politely gave blanket approval but made no business or artistic predictions for its future.[2]

The tune needed lyrics. Enter Kermit Goell.

The collaboration of Francis Craig and Kermit Goell was a fortunate passing of two ships in an artistic sea. The sum of their separate contributions to "Near You" was greater than its parts. Hybridization of their efforts on the song was analogous to the products of animal breeding in which mutts have unexpected strengths while purebreds break down from reinforcement of defects.

No two people could have been less alike. In contrast to the austere, Methodist, southern Craig of few interests, Goell was a Brooklyn-born son of well-off Russian-Jewish immigrants. He was extroverted, humorous, interesting, cosmopolitan, and quick. As manifested by multiple

Kermit Goell in the 1980s. (Courtesy of Bart Durham)

marriages and chronic financial tribulation, nonadmirers saw him otherwise—as an irresponsible, spoiled rascal. Lord Fauntleroy, meet Tom Brown.

In April 1946, Goell was travelling through Nashville to tout some of his songs. Nashville was a common stopover for composers because of WSM's national distribution of numerous shows, including Francis's. He met Francis while taking lunch in the Grill Room. After learning Goell was a lyricist, Francis played his new song for him. Though Goell thought the music "trite," he quickly penned lyrics for "Near You" onto a menu. He took the piece back to California, shelved it, and forgot it. He was, therefore, surprised to hear from Francis that autumn requesting a polished version of the lyrics suitable for recording. Goell sent back his original effort, unchanged. Why bother? [3]

Castle Recording's viability would be a milestone in the establishment of a self-sufficient Nashville music business. Previously the town had performers, a groundbreaking publisher, and high-powered radio dissemination. Now the missing (recording) link had been forged. No longer would local performers have to leave town to record their material. Technical, business, and artistic stars were now aligned.[4]

Two events assured that Castle would survive. The first was a recording session on December 11, 1946, for an obscure New York company called Sterling. The producer of that session was Fred Rose, one of the most influential people in Nashville music history. The performer was an undiscovered twenty-three year old singer/writer named Hank Williams. Songs recorded that day were "Calling You" and "Never Again Will I Knock on Your Door."[5] The second significant event for Castle was a session for Francis Craig's orchestra.

Francis assembled his orchestra for one of the last times for a recording session at WSM's Studio C on Monday evening, January 20, 1947. Owen Bradley produced the session for Bullet Records, the first ever produced by this man who had become a leading light in Nashville's music business. Aaron Shelton was the engineer, or mixer. The technology was relatively archaic; only three mikes were used. The audio signal was "piped" to the site of WSM's standby transmitter on Fifteenth Street and Weston, where the sixteen-inch "master" disk was cut on a lathe. The session seemed inadequately planned, and numerous partici- pants had deadlines. Union rules dictated that a maximum of four songs could be recorded in three hours. Bradley was committed to a dance job at the Andrew Jackson Hotel at 9:30.

No one had finally decided just what songs were to be recorded. Bulleit and Craig wanted to feature "Red Rose," the lovely tune recognized at least locally as Craig's theme. After recording that and two others, "Sometimes I Wonder" and "Hot Biscuits" (Bullet 1002), they still did not have a "B" (or "flip") side tune opposite "Red Rose." After hearing several nominees, Bulleit and Craig agreed on "Near You."

Aaron Shelton opined Francis wanted "Near You" because it featured a piano solo by the composer. That might have been ill advised, for Francis was rusty on the keyboard. He had fronted his orchestra rather than playing with it since the late twenties. The night before, he had auditioned "Near You" for Bulleit on NBC's *Francis Craig's Sunday Serenade*. Bob Lamm, a blind vocalist who had also played trumpet in the band since 1944, sang the refrain. On the air, Francis had forgotten the composed ending and quickly improvised a cute, syncopated gag signature. The arranger, Jim Hall, thought the ending "corny," but Bulleit liked it. Showing excellent musical instincts, he insisted it be used on the recording.

When it was time to record "Near You," Bradley had left for the Andrew Jackson. The musicians were tired but quickly rehearsed it a couple of times. Then they recorded it—perfectly. Bullet 1001-B was a take. The session ended at 10:00 P.M. The band remained at the station to play a local program at 10:30. It featured the just recorded "Near You." Interestingly, the orchestra used the original composed ending, not the one just recorded.

Jim Bulleit, founder of Bulleit Recording and Transcription Company. (From the Ragland Reporter, *October 1947)*

After its release on March 7, the local publicity push (for "Red Rose") began with a stunt. An airplane flew over downtown Nashville, dropping red roses onto the streets. Anyone bringing one of the roses to a record shop got a free record. The marketing gimmick produced a downtown traffic jam but few sales. "Red Rose" got some local jukebox play, but there did not appear to be even significant regional interest in the disk. The new Nashville independents had apparently laid an egg. Francis was crushed. His postlude resembled a dirge. Maybe it *was* all over.[6]

Then something unparalleled and wonderful occurred. A sleeper awoke. Overcoming tremendous odds, the flip side of "Red Rose" began to encroach on the public's ears. Though some attributed its sudden popularity to the "coin pushers" feeding jukeboxes, most believe the ascent of "Near You" began with a disk jockey in rural Georgia.

Cal Young was a twenty-five-year-old Nashvillian who had done some radio work in the military during World War II.

While working as a DJ at station WKEU in Griffin, Georgia, he came home for an April weekend. Being familiar with Francis Craig from his high school days and wanting to help his townsman, Young bought a copy of "Red Rose" to play on air in Griffin. Either he or one of his cohorts played the flip side, and strange events were set in motion. A few days later, the Record Heaven, a shop in the small town, called to buy a real inventory buster, one hundred copies of "Near You." Record Heaven had likely never placed such an order. Did the proprietors know something? Maybe not, but those ringing radio stations asking for "Near You" certainly did.

DJs around the South quickly picked up on the tune's popularity with their listeners. Hopscotching around the region, "Near You" in succession became number one in New Orleans, Birmingham, Atlanta, and St. Louis as summer ensued. It caught on relatively late in Nashville. The local spinners and listeners were enough interested in the more familiar "Red Rose" that they were late partaking the side that was hitting everywhere else. Young was one of the first to be mystified by the record's popularity and had no idea why it hit so big in Griffin. Considering what was happening, some statistician should have recognized Griffin as a very representative test market. The song it had pegged was about to move way beyond the South.

One of the first to recognize this was Jim Bulleit. His wife, Rachel, had said all along that the B-side might go somewhere. While driving to a South Carolina vacation in early summer, the Bulleits kept hearing "Near You" on the radio. As soon as they reached the beach, Bulleit received a frantic call from his staff to get back home and take care of a business problem he had never encountered, an overwhelming demand for one of his products. The vacation was aborted.

Bulleit could not keep up with orders. Despite using twenty-four record pressing plants around the nation, Bullet Recording by October got behind over six hundred thousand units. In addition to trying to satisfy customers, there was the problem of record bootleggers hustling out disks. Success was a two-edged sword. Better this though than uncertainty about whether the record business could survive in Nashville.[7]

The ultimate scorekeeper of any song's success was *Billboard*. Until 1954, that magazine used a combination of sheet music sales, jukebox sales, and air (radio) plays to tabulate rankings. 1947 had been a big year for independent record companies, Vitacoustic having scored earlier in the year with the Harmonicats' "Peg o' My Heart." In August, the magazine forecast good things for "Near You," identifying it as a local small-label "sleeper" with a potential for nationwide success. They thought Bullet Records might clean up. Typifying the obscurity of all parties associated with the project, writers called Francis Craig a "Mid-Western" bandleader with a local radio following. "Near You" was coming from nowheresville. Francis's ditty made the *Billboard* list in early August. It would be there a long, unprecedented time.[8]

Francis was elated. Fame and fortune had seemingly fallen from the sky onto the retiring, allegedly retired musician. Apparently the God of all grace had, after Francis's lifelong discipline, chosen to establish him (1 Pet. 5:10). Aaron Shelton and the production gang looked forward to redeeming a culinary dividend from Craig. He had promised that if the song ever made it to number one, he would take them all out for dinner at Jimmy Kelly's 216 Dinner Club and put a fifth of Jack Daniel's best (black label) whiskey at each of their settings. That promise was never fulfilled, though, as opportunity swept the new celebrity onto the national stage.[9]

Another improbability about the ranking ascent of "Near You" was that it occurred even before the song had been published. Sheet music sales were less important than in the past for a composition's commercial success. Every little bit helped though, and those sales were part of the trade tabulations. When he had recognized the potential of a bonanza, Francis had quickly hied off to New York and made the rounds of publication houses. Interest there was lukewarm. At Bregman-Vocco-Conn, he could not even get beyond the front office. He was, therefore, surprised on return home to have that house frantically calling him. They had apparently also recognized the boomlet and promised Craig they would make "Near You" their top plug if he would sign with them. He did.

It was published under one of the company's subsidiaries, Supreme Music Corporation.

The publisher quickly edited the song's ending. The original "hit" Francis Craig recording ended thus:

Make my wish come true,
By telling me that You
Want to spend the rest of your days
NEAR ME.

Francis agreed with the New "Yawk" publisher that things must be just right and agreed to end the song:

Make my life worthwhile,
By telling me that I'll
Spend the rest of my days
NEAR YOU.

The first major nonmusic publication to tell the wondrous story was *Newsweek*. The writer of a September 15 story noted that though Craig was a "Nashville institution," he was a national nonentity and that "Near You" had been produced on an unknown record label. Nashvillians were depicted as provincially proud that a song written and played by a southerner and recorded by a southern company had become a national hit. Wire service and columnist coverage (even Walter Winchell) soon followed.

By mid-October, *Billboard* called the success of "Near You" an unpredictable "freak happening" and graphically documented its amazing ride, which was not over. The song had been listed number one on August 30 in "Records

"Near You" sheet music cover.

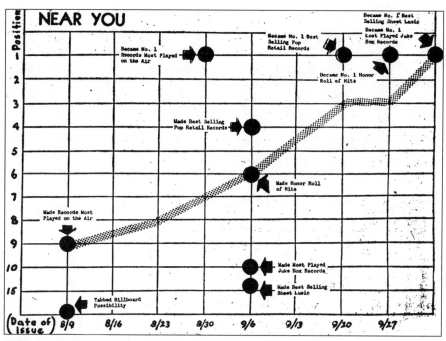

Billboard *graph, October 1947.*

Most Played on the Air" before it had even surfaced in other tabu-
lations. By September 6, it had appeared in other lists—those of
"Best-Selling Sheet Music," "Most-Played Juke Box Records,"
"Honor Roll of Hits," and "Best-Selling Popular Retail Records."
Having achieved first in all other categories, on September 27,
"Near You" became "No. 1" on the list that counted, the "Honor
Roll of Hits." It would stay in that position for seventeen consecu-
tive weeks, an all-time record! It eased down to number two on
December 27 and very gradually descended. It was not seen on
January 24, 1948, having been on the *Billboard* top-ten list for
twenty-five weeks.

The trade newspaper *Variety* also documented the rocket rise
and sustained popularity of "Near You." The song suddenly
appeared on the paper's "Top Talent and Tunes" list at the fifth
position on September 17. It was number one the following week
and stayed there for most of the rest of the year. "Near You" was
similarly listed on *Variety*'s machine music and sheet music lists.[10]

A performance arts ranking that made a more palpable, social splash back in Nashville was the appearance of "Near You" on *Your Hit Parade*. Sponsored by Lucky Strike cigarettes, this popular show was a Saturday night fixture on radio from its inception in 1935 to its television debut in 1950. In 1947, DJs had not become the dominant arbiter of song rankings, and the show was perceived by listeners as the truest determiner of what was best in popular music. Among the top-drawer singers belting out the top seven weekly hits in 1947 were Dinah Shore, Frank Sinatra, Martha Tilton, Dick Haymes, and Doris Day.

Excited family and friends held *Hit Parade* "listening parties" to exult in Francis Craig's ascent to stardom. Both teenage daughters, Celeste at Randolph Macon and Donia back home in Nashville, gathered around their radios with pals and Cokes to enjoy the show. Neither "Near You" nor Daddy let them down, though some traditionalists took umbrage at Sinatra's quasi-hillbilly rendition of the song on one show.

Francis Craig and the Andrews Sisters.

Starting on October 4, 1947, when it was number two, the song was broadcast fifteen consecutive weeks. Six of those weeks, "Near You" was number one.[11]

If imitation is the sincerest form of flattery, then Francis Craig must have been blushing. The quick recognition by professional musicians that there was something to "Near You" was dramatized by the many who rushed to "cover" the song just as soon as Craig's version hit the airwaves. "Near You" was recorded promptly by the Andrews Sisters, Larry Green, Alvino Rey, Elliot Lawrence, Frankie Laine, Victor Lombardo, the Auditones, and Dick (Two-Ton) Baker. To complete the musical spectrum, Lonzo and Oscar did a comedy, country version that became very popular. Everyone was eager to participate in "the musical miracle of 1947." Apparently no one could mess up the song. Its penetration transcended arrangement or artist. In addition to Craig's rendition, three or four of the covers were listed among the top fifteen in several categories—records most heard on the air, retail record sales, and jukebox plays.[12]

"Near You" was similar to a tune one cannot quit whistling, only in this case the obsession was a national phenomenon. Collegians universally declared it their favorite song. The title was drawn wafting out of radios in the comic strips "Harold Teen" and "Smilin' Jack." There was even a comic strip rendition in a music magazine about Craig's improbable breakthrough. At a special concert at the Ryman Auditorium, the announcer described the song's ubiquitousness. "Everywhere you go, 'Near You' is either sung, played, or fried in deep fat." WSM performers then proceeded to present Hawaiian, country, and operatic versions of the hit.

Not that he was trying, but Bill Kennon could not escape the song on the sidewalks of New York. During his otolaryngology residency, as he walked each morning down seedy Fourteenth Street past Union Square on the way to the New York Eye & Ear Hospital, Bill constantly heard "Near You" coming from still-open bars. He was reminded again of his native Nashville as he headed home in the evenings. Francis's song was still oozing from the same bars' jukeboxes. Through the autumn, the song was number one in jukebox plays in all parts of the country.[13]

"Near You" dominated the airwaves even in the comics.

FRANCIS CRAIG, SUPERSTAR

Francis Craig was now a commodity, not as a bandleader but as the composer and recorder of "Near You." Whether from his own volition or as an inevitable consequence of "Near You" mania, he became a solo showman, a star. By late September, the William Morris Agency had signed him for a six-month national tour. Bob Lamm was to be part of the act, which opened at the Hippodrome Theater in Baltimore. In addition to cementing his reputation, Francis stood to make some real money in the process. The agency was asking $2,500 per week for the act. Lamm was thought to be getting two hundred of that, not bad for the times but nowhere near what Craig was to receive, estimated to be more than $50,000 for the tour.[14]

Florence Lamm accompanied her husband. Elizabeth Craig stayed home with Donia. They played most of the major cities, from Boston in the East to Atlanta in the South to San Francisco on the West Coast. There were side trips to less metropolitan locales such as Sun Prairie, Wisconsin, and Lynchburg, Virginia, where Celeste's Randolph-Macon College mates were entertained.

Francis seemed to take on a new personality. Absent the burden of managing musicians, he seemed comfortable in a new role as soloist. Those knowing him as an introspective automaton might not have believed he could be so relaxed and convivial. Yankees had difficulty understanding his dialect but admired his gentlemanly qualities.

His aw-shucks naiveté was continually appreciated. He had a photographer snap a picture of his billing at one theater "for the family back in Nashville." He said one of his biggest show business thrills was seeing his name in lights at the Loew's Theater in New York after having helped so many others get to Broadway.

Craig's Southern traits were attractive, and he used that distinctiveness to the hilt, playing on the supposedly unexpected Southern success described by *Newsweek*. He was just being himself but probably recognized how old-fashioned he must have seemed to his audiences, especially above the Mason-Dixon Line. After an interview with Lauren Norvell of the *Atlanta Journal,* Norvell asserted, "Your life story should make a good film, Mr. Craig, since it would be the story of a southerner who hit the bigtime without leaving the South." How nice . . .

Craig with his vocalist Bob Lamm and Lamm's wife, Florence. (Courtesy Blair School of Music display)

One of his backstage visitors in New York was Jimmy Melton. His pal wondered if Francis still did a favorite old novelty number of playing "Dixie" with one hand and "Yankee Doodle Dandy" with the other. When

Oriental (Chicago) Theater marquee. (Courtesy of Donia Craig Dickerson)

Francis said he had been using it some on the tour, Melton told him not to use the hokey routine in his upcoming show in Boston. His brother, Edward, had also advised him that "all those Irish" would not appreciate the bit. Disregarding their advice, Francis "brought down the house" with the routine. He probably was not surprised. An early order for forty thousand records from Boston had heralded the "Near You" bonanza. He also saw the gimmick as a symbolic North-South reconciliation.

In November, Elizabeth and Donia visited the homesick Francis in Chicago, where he was doing five shows per day at the Oriental Theater, seven on Sunday. They had a wonderful time and returned loaded with anecdotes. When a cabbie learned that Elizabeth's spouse was the famous Francis Craig, he refused to charge her. In the theater, the Craig ladies politely but firmly corrected an attendee who insisted Bob Lamm could not possibly be blind. They had very personal knowledge that he was.

Craig and Lamm were usually second or third on a bill with a bigger name and a movie. They shared the stage with Gene

Krupa, Ella Fitzgerald, and Blue Barron. Critics generally gave high marks to the short (about twelve minutes) act, which consisted of some patter delivered in Francis's marked drawl, "Near You" with and without vocal, and Lamm's rendering "Margie" or "Stardust" vocally and on trumpet. They also frequently played a new song that was well received, "Beg Your Pardon." A Baltimore reviewer called Craig's piano style "a peculiar combo of hillbilly and (Carmen) Cavalero. . . ." Several thought that their performance was unpolished, even amateurish. However, the consensus was that this was a positive, demonstrating Craig's honesty and genuineness.[15]

Francis and Beasley Smith had written "Beg Your Pardon" and already sold it to a publisher. Francis had been quietly shilling the song throughout the tour, discussing it in interviews and beginning to perform it by December. He even used it on the *Spike Jones Show*, in which Jones introduced Francis as the three-in-one man, the writer, performer, and promoter of "Near You." In a Hollywood interview late in the tour, Francis explained that "Beg Your Pardon" was a polite "down South" phrase. The song was enough like "Near You" to be the big hit's little brother—same beat, arrangement, and danceability. Though not necessarily predictive of how the song would do, a perceptive New York reviewer of Francis's theater show noted it was "barely distinguishable" from "Near You." He also recommended that Francis "not try to carbon himself ad infinitum."

"Beg Your Pardon" appeared on *Billboard*'s "Picks" list, a presentation of likely successful

Bill with Gene Krupa.

Bill with Ella Fitzgerald.

recent releases, on December 27. The reviewer said that sequels rarely succeed but that this one had a chance. It made the same list the following month, prompting accolades for a version of it by the Dinning Sisters. In the same issue that "Near You" disappeared from the Honor Roll of Hits list, January 24, 1948, "Beg Your Pardon" made it at number ten. The Francis Craig version (Bullet 1012) was listed along with covers by the Dinning sisters, Frankie Carle, and Larry Green. Various pop music experts asserted that this was the first time a "follow-up" on a hit had become so successful.[16]

Francis was on an incredible winning streak. One of his tunes had set a *Billboard* duration record, and another was climbing the list. Dorothy Kilgallen called "Near You" the best record of 1947. *Billboard* selected it as the second top tune of the year. Despite much greater sales and air playtime, it trailed "Peg o' My Heart." In *Time* magazine's summary of the 1947 music year, they gave Bullet a left-handed compliment, saying that "Near You" had propelled a "dime-a-dozen" record company into big money.

The momentum of "Near You" was not over though, as it began a spring 1948 climb to number one in both record and sheet sales in Britain. Francis's orchestra was the third top-selling one of 1947, despite having just one record on the market. Only the orchestras of Vaughn Monroe and Ted Weems had sold more records than Francis Craig's. One year after its release, "Near You" had sold over two million three hundred thousand copies, a record for that time.

"Beg Your Pardon" was keeping the maestro in the public eye. It would climb as high as third on the Honor Roll of Hits and be on the chart a total of twenty weeks—no "Near You," but not bad. There was still reason to have listening parties back in Nashville. Beginning February 28, 1948, "Beg Your Pardon" was featured eleven straight weeks on *Your Hit Parade*. It got as high as third on five occasions but never made the top slot. Its first-year record sales would top one million.[17]

The tour extended to almost eight months, and Francis was tired of it. He wanted to enjoy some of the fruits of his new wealth, including a spanking new two-tone blue Cadillac. He had bought the car before going on tour and had bragged so much about it in Boston to Ella Fitzgerald, with whom he related well, that she went out and bought herself one. Now he used that vehicle to take Elizabeth and Celeste on a long-promised Florida vacation. Before heading south, Francis was presented a resolution from the Nashville City Council for his "Meritorious Service to Nashville and the State of Tennessee."[18]

In addition to visiting family and friends such as Howard Baughman in Florida, Francis did some successful deep-sea fishing. Apparently unready to give up his new career, he also did some radio and newspaper interviews, in which he began pushing his new single, "Foolin'" (Bullet 1013). Somewhere along the way, he had found time to cut this as well as "Beg Your Pardon." They were apparently done with the WSM staff orchestra, as Francis's band had scattered.[19]

Craig continued to garner awards. Perhaps the recognition of most personal satisfaction was a congratulatory phone call from Irving Berlin. There were other more tangible accolades. *Cash Box*, the publication of the jukebox industry, gave him a Special Award for his outstanding recording achievements. Most prestigious of all, The American Society of Song Writers gave him its Cleff Award for the outstanding song of 1947. This was the equivalent of today's Grammy award for a year's best song. "Near You" was the best.

Several acquaintances from the post-"Near You" time thought Francis was a tad ingenuous about his place in the music pantheon. Though never overbearing, he was noticeably proud of his great accomplishment. Patricia (Goell) Newcastle recalled Francis's visiting the Goells in Los Angeles as the "Near You" boom was diminishing. When Kermit told Francis about a studio

The *American Society of Song
Writers' Cleff Award was the equiva-
lent of today's Grammy Award.
(Courtesy of Donia Craig Dickerson)*

executive calling to wonder about using their song as a theme, Craig said, "I always knew they would want to make a story about myself." Newcastle insisted this was not an example of his subtle sense of humor.[20]

A haughty spirit does precede a fall, however (Prov. 16:18). If Craig's perception of his worth was inflated, reality rudely reduced his hat size. The momentum of his professional revival completely stalled after "Beg Your Pardon." For a short time, he kept plugging away. He made ten records for four labels after "Beg Your Pardon" (see discography).[21] Some of them were quaint and interesting. Capitalizing on a cameo appearance playing the bones on a Red Foley hit, "Alabama Jubilee," Craig issued "Play Them Bones," for Decca in 1952. Most of the latter arrangements, however, were repetitions of "Near You" and "Beg Your Pardon." Both of those had been definitely dated, a talented look backward, not forward. None after the successful two came close to getting on the charts.

As he approached old age, Francis settled back into the semiretirement anticipated for him in 1947 before he decided to leave a musical offering to his grandchildren. "Near You" was the capstone that almost obliterated the underlying edifice of his career, causing many to overlook all else he had done.

MEANING OF IT ALL

There was no recording industry in Nashville prior to 1946. The founders of Castle Studio almost single-handedly corrected that deficit in what otherwise was already a music entertainment and business center. The recording of

"Near You" launched Castle's reputation. In addition to being one of the first big hits done by any independent company, it was the first national hit out of Nashville.

Shortly after its inception, Castle moved its operation to the Tulane Hotel on North Eighth and Church Streets and began a sensational seven years of recording. Several important pop stars such as Rosemary Clooney and Ray Anthony were recorded, but most of their customers were the country musicians, who enjoyed staying home to plate their songs. In addition to the sensational Hank Williams's songs, they recorded Red Foley, Kitty Wells, Jimmie Dickens, and Ernest Tubb for MGM, Capitol, and Columbia. One year near the end of its tenure, Aaron Shelton estimated that Castle recorded 65 percent of *Billboard*'s Honor Roll of (country) Hits.

Some of their most interesting recordings were advertisements. One of the first was for jeweler Harold L. Shyer—or, in regional dialect, Harul Eul Shyuh. Shyer requested Snooky Lanson to sing his jingle. Snooky felt such work below him and tried to price himself out of the gig, demanding five hundred dollars for it. The jeweler immediately took him up on it, and they made an ad that seemed to run interminably in Nashville.

All this brought some notoriety but little money to the founders. They had plowed all their earnings back into the business and did not make any significant profits. Charges to their customers were not expensive—approximately one hundred dollars per three-hour session. Their venture ended in 1954 when Edwin Craig decided that WSM employees had to devote all their time to the station or leave it. The middle-aged engineers who had founded Castle Recording Laboratory were of modest means, needed security and benefits, and were overworked trying to serve WSM and their exciting new business. Additionally, television was coming to Nashville through WSM, a process in which Aaron Shelton would be greatly involved. They closed down Castle after pioneering the recording industry in Nashville. Two other prominent employees, Jack Stapp and Jim Denny, chose to leave WSM in the purge in order to found two important music publishing houses, Tree Publishing and Cedarwood Publishing respectively.

Competition had started to develop even before Castle closed. In 1950, Capitol Records became the first of the majors to establish a Nashville office. Owen Bradley, now Decca's A & R man in Nashville, and his brother Harold had two other recording studios before building their famous Quonset hut on Sixteenth Avenue in 1955, beginning what would come to be known as Music Row. RCA, under operations manager Chet Atkins, located in Nashville in 1957. The rush was on. By 1963, half of all American records were produced in Nashville.[22]

Ironically, the hit that announced to the nation that Nashville was a new recording alternative to New York or Los Angeles was not a hillbilly cut. It is far-fetched to say this would not have happened without Francis Craig's "Near You." Castle had demonstrated its capability with the Hank Williams records. Country musicians were ecstatic and ready to do their recordings at home, and most of Nashville's later product would be their work. However, this music did not then have the national market that pop did. Francis could not have imagined when he recorded "Near You" that it would be a catalyst to kick-start the Nashville recording industry. That, however, is precisely what it was.[23]

Roger Kinkle thought that the quality of songwriting deteriorated after World War II, approximately contemporaneous with the demise of big bands. There is little doubt that the poetry in lyrics disappeared, more supposedly insightful generations preferring ostensibly deeper messages to those of romance and fun. Still, Kinkle's indictment of the total popular music product is obviously an opinion, and a song creating the impact of "Near You" cannot be so broadly dismissed. Kinkle's own listing of representative recordings of 1947 had some songs which remained popular over the years, including "Stella by Starlight," "Ballerina," "Now Is the Hour," "That's My Desire," "Mam'selle," and "Almost Like Being in Love."[24]

In the recording era, "Near You" was the biggest ever short-term pop single. Its run of seventeen consecutive weeks as number one on the *Billboard* list, the most meaningful tabulation, remains a record; and its twenty-five weeks on the chart ranks among the highest. The kingpin of recurring sales was Irving Berlin's "White Christmas," introduced in 1942. It was the nation's number one song for fourteen weeks, though its chart listing over several years was sixty-three weeks. The remainder of the top ten sellers prior to 1954 all had thirteen-week runs at the top and included some songs perhaps more recognizable to current audiences than "Near You." They were "Frenesi" (1940), "My Blue Heaven" (1927), "Tennessee Waltz" (1950), "I've Heard That Song Before" (1943), "Goodnight, Irene" (1950), "Dardanella" (1920), "The Gypsy" (1946), and "Heartaches" (1947—a very good year).

Billboard's compilations were changed after 1954 when the "Hot 100" list became featured. Only store record sales and air play were used in the formula. The Honor Roll of Hits was discontinued in 1963. Preeminence by any particular song was diluted by a proliferation of categories. Since 1954, only one single has challenged the amazing run of Francis Craig's song. In 1995, Mariah Carey's "One Sweet Day" was first for sixteen consecutive weeks on the Adult Contemporary list.[25]

Numerous contemporaneous musicians and publications expressed incredulity about the phenomenal success of "Near You." Certainly its origin and dissemination were unique—composed by nationally minor players, performed by the tunesmith, recorded by a start-up independent label without Broadway or Hollywood roots, and (shet mah mouth!) being strictly Southern. Buyers are, however, more discriminating with their money, and all those unique features do not a hit make.

Opinions of modern composers and musicians relatively unfamiliar with "Near You" and its big success are telling. Layng Martine Jr. was impressed with its structure. Most three-part popular songs alternate verse and chorus with a bridge, an entirely different section preceding the last, familiar chorus. The classical pop tune structure is thus AABA. There was no bridge in "Near You." Rather the structure was ABAC, which Martine considered interesting and distinctive.[26]

Dale Cockrell thought the ABAC pattern within a typical thirty-two bars was not that unusual. Neither was it unusual not to record the little known verse of "Near You." By 1947, that technique was common in order to squeeze a song onto a seventy-eight rpm (revolutions per minute) record disk.

Cockrell liked the centrality of the song's words, especially the isolated syncopation of the words "Near You."[27]

The pianist, Beegie Adair, attempted playing "Near You" as a child and found the effort technically challenging. In reacquainting herself with his record, she felt Francis's keyboard work was good; he could "get around on the instrument." His licks, as at the song's end, were playful. The song reminded her of cute, technical numbers such as "Nola" or "Kitten on the Keys." The use of left-hand boogie-woogie was central to the song's charm. She thought his use of left-hand triplets was perhaps pace setting and wondered if Floyd Cramer had ever listened to him play. The "Nashville Sound" had not yet been invented when "Near You" was issued. Adair, however, said its arrangement was clearly not of New York or Los Angeles and opined that the 1947 listening public may have been discerning enough to appreciate that difference.[28]

Bob McDill, a composer of thirty number-one country songs, broke the song and record into several parts, finding some of them mundane and others excellent. He thought the lyrics "sweet and harmless," believing few records were bought because of them. The sound was also unimpressive, probably below average even for that time. Unlike some of the complimentary critics on Craig's and Lamm's tour, McDill also dismissed the vocal performance, finding it adequate at best, banal and off-pitch at worst. Conversely, Francis Craig's contribution was impressive. The melody was crisp and interesting. The riff seemed to have little relationship with the melody but constantly complimented it—a "yin and yang" relationship. The syncopated beat got the listener's attention and was "a perfect fox trot." The arrangement was intriguing. The alternation of solo piano and orchestra (with vocalist) playing the melody gave the impression of listening to different records. This reviewer's best kudos went to Francis's piano performance, which seemed light-hearted, crisp, and accurate—almost as if Francis were having lots of fun. McDill felt that the magic of "Near You" was still present after half a century.[29]

Knowing what it *was, is* it a "classic" or "standard" piece of music? As far as sales are concerned, it was pretty big. Again, the champ in this category was "White Christmas," which by 1954 had sold over thirty million sides. Staying with the holiday theme (always helpful to a clever composer), "Rudolph, The Red-Nosed Reindeer" was next at eight million. "Near You" was in the midst of eighteen others that sold over two million records—pretty good company!

"Near You" had remained popular enough through the early 1950s for Milton Berle to make it the closing theme song of his long-running television show, *Texaco Star Theater.* He apparently felt some proprietary affiliation with the song. When informed in a Hollywood restaurant by Nashvillian Bart Durham that his friend, Kermit Goell, had written the theme song, Berle expressed anger that the composer [*sic*] had never thanked him for his boosting the piece. "I made that song, and they never once thanked me." With typical show-biz chutzpah, Berle overlooked that Francis Craig had made a few waves with "Near You" several years before it was used on television.[30]

A decade after its release, "Near You" was not listed among the one hundred most recorded songs or among the thirty favorite all-time records among disk jockeys. Neither was it listed among the top songs used on the Hit Parade. It was suitable for revival though, surely a criterion for consideration as a standard. After 1947, it was covered by some well-known recording artists, including Roger Williams, Lamar Morris, Wayne King, Floyd Cramer, Roy Clark, Slim Whitman, and Nat Cole.

George Jones and Tammy Wynette, however, recorded the most smashing later cover. "Near You" had always lent itself to many kinds of arrangements. During a Nashville tenure in the 1980s, Kermit Goell persuaded the producer Billy Sherrill to use the song as a ballad. Sherrill had the brilliant, though star-crossed, duo record "Near You" in 1974. It was their last recording as husband and wife. The day after completing the cut, George left the house while Tammy was at the dentist's, and they soon divorced.

George and Tammy's "Near You" was done in the "Nashville Sound," a controversial arrangement style somewhere between country and pop that proved commercially successful.[31] The duet featured underlying sweet strings, a moaning pedal steel guitar and rhythm guitar up front, and, unlike earlier versions, a slow tempo (one hundred beats per minute). Released in late 1976, the disk appeared on the country charts on December 12, stayed there for sixteen weeks, and was number one for two weeks. Their dreamy version of Francis Craig and Kermit Goell's song was later heard easing from a tavern jukebox in the 1994 Paul Newman movie, "Nobody's Fool."[32]

No one knows what makes a hit. Otherwise, as Bob McDill noted, the best executive in the best company could probably then produce one a week. Hits are unscientifically created and depend on the subjective feelings they arouse in listeners. "Near You" was unequivocally a hit, whether judged by numbers sold or times overheard being whistled in the grocery store, and no one knows why. Perhaps Billy Rose, the Broadway producer, gave the pithiest analysis of its success when he declared it unexplainable, just like bubble gum and Dwight Eisenhower's popularity.[33]

A standard is ultimately determined not by numbers sold or played. Those criteria are measurements of initial success. Whether "Near You" is a standard depends on the evaluator. Unlike "My Blue Heaven," "Over the Rainbow," or "September Song," "Near You" would probably fail the challenge of being recognizable by most current piano-bar players. George Jones and Tammy Wynette showed that Francis's song has historic legs. True oldies radio stations will occasionally play original recordings of it. Perhaps, if given the chance, even currently tune-challenged fans of hip-hop, modern country, or numerous styles of rock music would conclude, as Francis Craig did, that "Near You" was natural and understandable, ". . . like a cool drink of water."[34] Applying necessarily nonscientific judgement, "Near You" surely ranks somewhere in the middle of the popular repertoire as a "standard."

CODA

Whether or not he intended it, this time Francis Craig's retirement was for real. After achieving fame, wealth, and good reviews on his "Near You" tour, he had responded to ambition's flame. The fruits of that stimulus produced an audience yawn. The public has always chosen musical hits for their distinctiveness and were apparently bored with Francis's attempted duplications of "Near You."

Francis now had time to write. The majority of his pieces were published after 1947. Similar to his records, he enjoyed no significant success with anything after "Beg Your Pardon" (see catalogue). He penned some pieces to satisfy local requests. Some of these were never published. In 1951, he wrote a rousing march to celebrate the seventy-fifth anniversary of the *Nashville Banner*. He helped the Girl Scouts in 1957 with "(Won't You Buy) Some Girl Scout Cookies?" In 1961, he wrote "Fly Our Flag Forever" for the local American Legion.[35]

Honors continued to come. Representative Percy Priest hosted a dinner for him given by the Tennessee State Society at the National Press Club in March 1952. Fame though was invariably fleeting, and he receded from the limelight.[36]

There were also the aggravations of notoriety, with which he was unfamiliar and extremely uncomfortable. He never imagined that his litigious land buzzed with flies anxious to profit from others' honey. One such surfaced from the left coast to challenge those associated with "Near You." Thelma H. Jones of California sued Supreme Music Corp. et al. for $150,000, alleging in 1951 in New York that when he wrote "Near You," Francis had plagiarized her copyrighted 1934 song "Just An Old Fashioned Mother and Dad." Not losing hope after that suit was dismissed, she sued Francis, himself, in federal court. Francis took all this personally, never accepting his barrister's reassurance that such aggravations were just part of doing business. Much to his relief, the federal suit was also dismissed in spring 1953.[37]

Francis continued to do some minor work at WSM as music librarian. Not all station executives were happy about creating a previously unneeded slot for the boss's cousin. He was so inconspicuous that some company contemporaries do not remember him being there. He never seemed busy and was always available for a cordial afternoon Coke break. He usually took lunch at the National Life cafeteria, where he enjoyed the company of old pals and family.

Craig joins in the singing at a Tennessee State Society party in March 1952. Left to right: *Congressmen Joe Evins, James Frazier Jr., Jere Cooper, and Percy Priest.*

His buddies continued to play jokes on Francis at lunch and other times. Ed Webb and some other executives thoroughly convinced him that he was to be named to the National Life Board on a particular date. After arriving groomed and in his best suit on the appointed day, he learned it was yet another ruse. Beasley Smith repeatedly led Francis on about the huge royalty checks he was getting from ASCAP. Francis's allotments were never in such amounts, and he wondered why. When Francis was touting his new car at a party at Jimmy Kelly's Restaurant, Webb urged everyone to convene outside so the proud owner could demonstrate his chariot. Webb had set him up by putting the rear axle on blocks. When Webb asked Francis to demonstrate the car, he could never figure out why it wouldn't go forward or backwards.

Francis would come home in the evening with his stomach tied in knots over some of these jokes, but he never saw them as a reason not to continue pleasurable social intercourse. Whatever his internal dynamics, externally he remained cordial, unaffected, and a welcome addition to comradely convocations. A participant in the National Life lunchtime klatches of that time called him "a Christian human being."[38]

Francis and Elizabeth enjoyed travel. They experienced danger and adventure on a trip to Europe in spring 1954. Out of New York, their Pan American airliner had to return to Idlewild Airport for an emergency landing because the plane's landing gear failed to retract. After finally getting to Germany, they received VIP treatment because Francis's brother, General Charles Craig, had just finished a tour as head of U.S. forces in Berlin. On the sealed train back through the Russian zone to West Germany, Francis and Elizabeth got an impromptu public blessing for his choice of careers made thirty years earlier. They overheard a couple talking about General Craig's brother, who had been the black sheep of his family until he wrote "Near You."[39]

For several years in the late fifties and early sixties, Francis had a classic, silver Airstream trailer. The couple wintered in Sarasota one season but did not make its use a recreational imperative. Francis's wife was tolerant of the toy, but there was something terribly incongruous about the elegant Elizabeth and trailer parks. After the trailer was finally parked behind their upscale Nashville home, they built a shuffleboard court beside it for their grandchildren's use.[40]

Commensurate with their backgrounds and personalities, Francis Craig and Kermit Goell did not have much to do with each other. In the midst of the "Near You" hysteria, Dorothy Kilgallen reported that Goell planned to sue Francis for "taking all the credit for the song," insisting he deserved a cut of the "vaudeville gold" Francis was getting on his tour. Through the years, he repeatedly whined that Francis got too many of the honors for the song, forgetting that the composer also had a hit record with it. When Francis's widow had a conversation with the lyricist about his refrain of envy, she wondered in an austere, typically polite manner if "Mr. Goell" were not getting his royalty checks on time. Touché!

Goell spent most of the 1980s in Nashville, writing for the country market. Among his more successful songs were "Shepherd Serenade," "Slowly," "Cajun Born," and "Huggin' and Chalkin.'" He ended with an ASCAP list of 104. None approached "Near You" in wallop or remuneration. He died in 1998.[41]

Just as Craig and Goell, many of the other principals who made the record soon faded. Castle Recording ended in 1954. Perhaps more surprising were the rise and fall of Bullet Recording.

"Near You" provided the financial stake that allowed Jim Bulleit to get underway. His wife, Rachel, called it "manna from heaven." In an apparent attempt to cover the recording waterfront, Bulleit developed gospel, sepia ("race"), country, popular, and a small Mexican series of recordings. Some of the performers were prominent. In the gospel group were Wally Fowler and the Speer Family. He was particularly influential in providing opportunity for black performers in music. Sepia recorders included the Fairfield Four, Cecil Gant, and B. B. King. Chet Atkins made his first solo record, "Guitar Blues," for Bullet Recording. Other prominent country artists gracing the label were Clyde Moody, Pee Wee King, and Ray Price. In addition to Francis Craig, transient pop artists included Bob Crosby, Les Elgart, and Bob Troup. In 1948, Bullet opened Nashville's first record-pressing facility. Apparently with a gold mine of his own innovation, Jim Bulleit called his business "the fastest growing independent record co. in America."

Bulleit was a hustler but was over his head in the recording industry. He always resented the numerous hands dipping into the till of projects. He was also a poor manager and spent far beyond his company's means to entertain musicians and other role players in the sometimes shady music business. The probable basis for his finally failing was recording far more losers than hit makers among the more than one thousand sides Bullet released. By the mid-fifties, the IRS was calling on Mr. Bulleit, and he was forced to declare bankruptcy. Jim Bulleit had shown that an independent could make it and that he could just as easily fail in this risky business. He died in 1988.[42]

In the early 1960s, Francis learned of a woodsy lot for sale in Sewanee, Tennessee—ninety miles southeast of Nashville in the Cumberland Mountains, home of the University of the South, and a site of traditional summer retreat for parched Nashvillians. Again, Elizabeth was not too enthusiastic about her husband's idea. They were in their sixties and ensconced in Nashville, their married home for over thirty-five years. Francis, though, thought Nashville was becoming uncomfortable for him.

He had a point. The city was booming. Enlightened Nashville and Davidson County leaders had shepherded through a metropolitan form of government in 1963, ameliorating schisms that would plague other areas. Just as it had in previous centuries been blessed by outstanding central water and rail access, Nashville was now a hub of the new Federal Interstate Highway System. Bank clearings had increased 93 percent in the most recent decade. Assessed property values were up 66 percent. Population had increased 67 percent, far outstripping the state and nation. Between 1920, about when Francis established himself in Nashville, and 1965, the Nashville-Davidson County population had increased 176 percent.

Though there is no record of his opinion on such matters, social (mainly racial) ferment had come to Nashville along with the rest of the nation. The "Nashville Plan" for school integration was deemed enlightened by some, but local blacks and the federal government did not approve of its gradualism. Along with their counterparts in Greensboro, North Carolina, black Nashville collegians had in 1960 led a peaceful revolt against segregation at lunch counters.

This was no longer the manageable town Francis Craig remembered from his college days through his career. Though Nashville was go-go, Francis was gone-gone. Family and friends had noted slowing of his cognitive faculties. The old maestro was unable to cope with all this change. He was only being instinctively self-protective to want to get out of town.[43]

Just outside Sewanee, the Craigs built a unique, rustic-appearing, yet elegant home that overlooked through a panoply of picture windows in its back a deep, forested valley called Lost Cove. Featuring two steepled sections, the house's facade was of stained, wide, vertical planks with a skirt of native sandstone around its lower quarter. Yet another Phi Delta Theta, Charles Waterfield Jr., designed it. The architect was the son of one of Craig's fraternity mates. The Tennessee Alpha Phis truly were their brothers' keepers (Gen. 4:9). Francis and Elizabeth moved there in summer 1966.

Their time together there was too brief. While enjoying an afternoon autumn view of the cove from the back deck of this spanking new retirement home, Francis Craig was stricken with a heart attack. He was cared for at a little infirmary in Sewanee and was stable enough to visit with his family for much of the forty-eight hours before he died quietly on November 19, 1966. He was buried in Nashville's Mt. Olivet Cemetery.

Three weeks before his death, Francis and Elizabeth had joined a formal party commemorating Belle Meade Country Club's fiftieth anniversary. Craig's admirers had cajoled him to

Francis Craig at the keyboard, Belle Meade Country Club, October 1966. (Courtesy of Donia Craig Dickerson)

once more play "Near You," the song that had provided his lasting reputation and awakened the nation that Nashville was now the new kid on the recording industry block. As he had done innumerable times since 1923, Francis sat at the ivories and entertained a bunch of Southern socialites with sedately swinging music. He marveled at the enthusiastic, tearful ovation he inspired, expressing abashment that they could have enjoyed his work that much. In the quiet of retirement, away from dancers, microphones, and packed work schedules, he had forgotten what he had meant to his city. His status was defined by an editorialist, who said of this maestro known as much for his gentlemanliness as his musicianship—"No orchestra leader or composer on the local scene has been longer or more popularly identified with Nashville. . . ."

In the midst of numerous letters of condolence to Francis Craig's family was one from the collaborator who helped create the lasting reputations of both of them. Kermit Goell wrote Elizabeth that, "To create something lovely and lasting is something for which one must thank God, who has his hand in all creativity."[44]

AND NOW...

In 1999, Francis Craig's version of music was at least discernable on the popular market. A resurgence of interest among college students in that archaic form of socially acceptable rhythmic relation, ballroom dancing, bode well for a revival of swing. The Bill Elliot Swing Orchestra most closely emulated their musical ancestors of sixty years previous. Other groups, such as Squirrel Nut Zippers, Big Bad Voodoo Daddy, and Cherry Poppin' Daddies (in spite of crude lyrics), sounded like dance bands. The Bill Holman and Gerald Wilson orchestras could best be characterized as jazz symphony orchetsras. Brian Setzer's recordings were still listed under the rock category and were very popular.

These bands had their own distinctive sounds but differed from their swing ancestors in some obvious general ways. They rarely had as many musicians—few lush sax sections here. Their music understandably included some of the rock and jazz created since the first swing era. Their sounds were consistently louder, usually augmented by electronics. Tempos were more insistent; ballads were scarce in their libraries. Whether for consideration of taste or (more likely) business, the bands usually played compositions by members of their organizations. They did not recognize there might be a classic popular repertoire.

Thus true believers thought swing had only been resting and would again dominate the popular music scene. Discussants and marketers addressing the revival larded their communications with the prefixes retro- or neo-. More skeptical observers had noted several unfulfilled prophecies of its return and doubted any resurgence.[45]

After the onslaught of television, the eight-hundred-pound-entertainment gorilla, and FM radio, WSM-AM receded in influence. WSM's The Waking Crew Orchestra was the last live radio studio orchestra in the United States. It ceased along with its immensely enjoyed early morning show on March 15, 1983. By 1999, WSM-AM had an entirely country music and news format and was the tenth most listened-to station in Nashville. The only remnant of its years of influence was the endurance of the *Grand Ole Opry*.[46]

The Hermitage Hotel survived hard times in the last quarter of the century. Deemed unsafe for occupancy, Metropolitan officials shut it down in 1977. Numerous Nashville government and business interests recognized its historic importance, its central location, and a promising future. Thanks to the Metropolitan Historical Commission, it was placed on the National Register of Historic Places. Thanks in part to the financing of Metropolitan revenue bonds, the hotel was refurbished and reopened in 1980. After several false starts and owners, the hotel was thriving in 1999 as a part of the Westin chain. Management did not feature live music on a regular basis.[47]

By 1995, the annual dollar value of Nashville recordings had exceeded two billion dollars. In 1996, there were 248 recording studios and ninety-six record labels in Nashville. In a plusher economic environment and with different marketing techniques, modern country stars such as Garth Brooks and Shania Twain realized album sales of over ten million. The industry was shaken

Elizabeth Craig Lancaster makes a point to Vice President George Bush on the occasion of his receiving an honorary doctorate in Civil Law from the University of the South, 6 October 1985. (Courtesy of Donia Craig Dickerson)

in early 1999 by consolidation, loss of jobs, and disappearance from Nashville of Decca Records, a company so central to its music history. Most analysts considered this only a bump in the road for the recording center. A surprising result of industry rearrangement was the reemergence of independent labels.[48]

Elizabeth Gewin Craig made a new and satisfying life after Francis's death. The widow had inherited a healthy estate, somewhere between one-half and one million dollars, a good bit of money in 1966. She worked at the music listening area of the DuPont Library of the University of the South from 1967–1980. The listening complex of the library was named for her when she retired from this activity. She married Dr. Robert Lancaster, a widower and longtime dean and development director at the University of the South in 1980. The Craigs and Lancasters had been friends. Her proud second husband described her as ". . . a woman of beauty and wit, of splendid character and never-failing compassion." She expressed genuine gratitude for the blessing of "two wonderful husbands."[49]

ripresa

Recapitulation

Francis Craig was a man of glaring paradoxes. These conflicts abounded in his personal, social, and professional lives. He was very private; if he ever discussed such dichotomies, it would have been in the most intimate of councils. As he never seemed to recognize any of them, he remained a quandary to most people relating to him, resulting in divergent opinions of his intellect, accomplishments, and value. In appraising Craig, one person's perceived arrogance and snobbishness were another's good taste and politeness.

It is unclear whether Francis and his family were universally comfortable with the confusing socioeconomic paradox in their lives. To many musicians and most of his public, he was a "rich man," an aristocrat dabbling in music even though he really did not need to in order to make a living. That was not the reality. The Nashville *bona fides* of Phi Delta Theta, Vanderbilt, and the Craig name did not obviate the facts that, due to Father Craig's eschewing the opportunity proffered by his brothers, Francis began poor and achieved security only by working very hard at a risky and, to some, unrespectable business. When Elizabeth's family lost their wealth in the Depression, the Francis Craigs had no financial cushion whatsoever. Their refinement would not pay the bills, and Francis, to his credit, more than fulfilled his role as provider.

The Craigs were not a part of the local social swirl, a circumstance that Elizabeth had enjoyed in Birmingham. Membership in the most important clubs, such as Atlanta's Piedmont Driving Club and Nashville's Belle Meade Country Club, had been a status symbol in the New South since the Civil War.[1] Whatever the opportunities for sport, business, and relationships with folks of like stripe, membership in Belle Meade Country Club was also definitely recognized by Nashville's social elite as a badge of arrival and acceptability. Francis Craig *worked* at the Club. Regardless of his affability and kinship with partyers, for two decades he was the man on the bandstand—seemingly at one with the celebrants, yet still their employee. He joined Belle Meade Club after World War II as he approached retirement. Having achieved status and security, this act probably had less symbolic meaning than it earlier might have. Who knew, though, what lurked behind his inscrutable façade.

Francis was convivial with his musical peers but only marginally comfortable with his employees. An observant participant in the popular music business said there are two very distinct types of bandleaders. The first has a sense of humor, enjoys the company of mostly carefree musicians, and serves as a buffer between his players and the band's employers. The second is more management oriented and may take advantage of the players—or at least be perceived to do so. He is more interested in the business of the band than the joy of making music through it. Francis was clearly the latter type.

He was tough enough but never adjusted to the varieties of musician personalities—some straight, some kooky. Many were drinkers and pursued lifestyles opposite that of their unblemished and disapproving boss. One of his intemperate trumpet players kept his toddy in his straight mute. His employees' mischievousness toward him was in the spirit of clean fun but was also a passive-aggressive response to polite but distant management. It was more than the usual worker grousing. The "so square" gentleman was just very different from them, and they sought to ruffle his feathers. Though he usually chuckled at the tricks, they also unsettled him. He was not so impervious that he could not detect their purpose.[2]

Just as his father did, those knowing Francis must have continually asked why he chose the work he pursued. As one of the long-time, observant WSM employees wondered, "How did Francis ever get into music?" His sedate personality seemed inappropriate for a popular bandleader. He was without stage charisma and had to let the music, fortunately very good, speak for itself. He never spoke on his national radio shows, preferring to let the announcers bask in the auditory spotlight. Those touting the Craig orchestra's preeminence in the South had to compare its work to Kay Kyser's group.[3] The music of the two bands, one from Tennessee the other from North Carolina, was not that different. The clear difference was Kyser's striking stage personality, of which Francis was devoid. If he ever experienced *joie de vivre*, it was not expressed in his public performances.

He was an ethical duck out of water in the music business. As Kermit Goell's son observed from watching his father, the minority of people in the music business make a real living and those who do have to have a bit of rascal about them.[4] Yet, his father was a clever rascal and rarely made ends meet, while the honest Francis Craig succeeded financially, even before "Near You."

Critics might accuse him of being a beneficiary of nepotism; but, once afforded an opportunity by his family, he had to deliver, and he did. They never accused him though of bribery. Chicanery in pushing one's musical product had always been a virtue in the music business. The public paid attention to that shady side of where their favorite tunes came from only in the 1950s when the federal government got interested in the reasons why certain songs were being played on the air. The so-called Payola scandal came well after "Near You." Cal Young insisted his first spinning the song was by choice, not persuasion. There is no evidence that Francis ever paid anyone off for anything. His moral barometer and the security accruing from his good work kept him serenely above the sometimes illegal or immoral pitfalls of his chosen business.[5]

Something stirred in his breast to overcome all these impediments and become a popular musician. Perhaps the instrumental versions of "Near You" and "Beg Your Pardon" were meaningful metaphors for personal struggles that were never resolved. Francis's description of "Near You"—and most subsequent recordings were like it—was that the right hand had a "Dixie" flavor and the left was boogie-woogie. He claimed he got the arrangement idea from an Art Tatum recording. There was really nothing distinctively Dixieland about the right hand. Perhaps this was just another characterization to reinforce the southern flavor he constantly sought to convey. The right hand played an uncomplicated, mildly syncopated, probably forgettable

Francis Craig and bandleader Kay Kyser.

melody. Like his song, how interesting was a buttoned-up, inscrutable, preacher's son, who emulated aristocracy and was most charming at intimate dinner parties?

The left hand, though, was another matter. It muttered an *ostinato*, jazz rhythm popularized by black musicians and occasionally hammered out some rough, attention-grabbing, perhaps precedent-setting triplets. The southpaw was clearly attached to a guy who was initially musically seduced by ragtime and, for heaven's sake, enjoyed playing the *bones*. Now that may have been a little raffish, but it was interesting.

The right hand usually dominates, though, on the piano and in life. In psychological terms, Francis Craig's superego almost always prevailed over his id. His image was in contrast to that expected of a popular bandleader and in tune with his cultured background and the upper crust social set with which he seemed most comfortable. Despite the glimmer of color in his recordings of both the twenties and forties, his music remained staid. He was more the leader than a performer throughout his career, so his piano work was dated and not risky—preferably in the key of G. He played what one of his musicians called a "parlor piano."

He would have been confused by all such analysis and was surely correct in following his instincts into a career that became highly successful. If asked to explain why such a person as he would pursue such an unlikely calling, he would likely have provided the same typically brief but probably correct conclusion his wife reached, that he "just had rhythm."[6]

Francis was a devoted family man and must have looked back on his provision for them as the highlight of his adult life. Beyond that very personal accomplishment, he did some important things in his profession. Most of those sprang not from extraordinary talent but tenacity and facility. When there was work, he kept at it. He quickly recognized opportunities and took advantage of them. Not an academician, college for him was only good for a touch of polishing and, more important, for making contacts. The evolution of dance bands, hotel orchestras, and radio came in the early 1920s, when he was failing at Vanderbilt. There was no precedent for any of these phenomena in his youth. Against family wishes and sensible advice, he quickly took advantage of opportunities in those brand new fields. The Craig contacts helped, but his family would surely have felt better had he accepted an also-offered career in the insurance business.

Francis followed his muse, making him a happier man (though he seldom demonstrated that), an economic success, and a pacesetter. His orchestra was generally considered the *best* in Nashville. He played on the *first* WSM broadcast. His much-admired tenure at the Hermitage Hotel was the *longest* anyone could recall at any hotel. "Near You" was *Billboard*'s consecutive number one single recording *longer* than any other before or since.

"Near You" unexpectedly made his reputation beyond the South. Aside from the inexplicable reasons why this song hit so big, there was also no reason why it should have flowed from Craig's brain and hands. He did not work hard at songwriting and was not prolific at the craft. Neither did he spend much time on musical arrangements. Contrary to what some admirers have asserted, the song did not come from a moment of genius. "Near You" seemed the instinctive product of a person who had diligently pursued his trade, a yield of perspiration rather than inspiration. If a musician were blessed with good inner "rhythm" (perhaps another word for talent), something good might happen after working through two generations of pop music and playing hundreds of dances. It did.

Francis Craig was not a religious or introspective man. Whether because of his late Saturday nights at work or in reaction to the possibly suffocating religion of his youth, he was only a sporadic attender at the West End Methodist Church. There is no evidence he ever pondered in depth the tenets of Methodism. As the founder of the Anglican evangelical wing of the Methodist Church, John Wesley disagreed with John Calvin on many matters, particularly predestination. One principle they agreed on though was the concept of one's calling. In order to create a harmonious earthly community, Calvin preached, and Wesley agreed, that the faithful could best aid others by exercising their particular talents.

Francis Craig probably never mused on the idea but uncannily recognized his calling—the production of a certain type of popular music. He pursued this paradoxical subliminal summons with most of the virtues taught by his church through his parents—industry, thrift, and domestic order. He was a good man who used his capability to its utmost. For the fruits of those labors, his family and fans, Southern and otherwise, could be forgiven the deadly sin of pride (Prov. 16:18).[7]

CHAPTER SIX

There's just one place for me, NEAR YOU.

graduati del orchestra

Craig Orchestra Graduates

Francis Craig did not single-handedly make the career of any of the numerous musicians who achieved stardom after working with his orchestra. He did not even get along with some of them. However, his proven capacity to recognize and hire good talent said reams about all parties of the employment equation. His orchestra was an established, excellent one, and talented performers saw an opportunity in working with him. In addition to regular employment, one could anticipate good exposure, especially through WSM, and a chance to move on up in the entertainment business. The so-called graduates were an important part of Francis Craig's product and career, both while with him and later when they spread his fame along with their own. In chronological order, they included:

IRENE BEASLEY

Irene Beasley was a twenty-one-year-old Sweet Briar–educated junior high teacher in Memphis in 1925, when she began commuting to Nashville to appear on weekend WSM broadcasts with Francis Craig. It was rare for orchestras to feature girl singers at the time. By 1928, she was appearing regularly on Memphis radio. After a further apprenticeship in Chicago, she went to New York in 1929 and was signed by Columbia Broadcasting System. The "long, tall gal from Dixie" was featured on numerous radio shows and was voted "Queen of Radio" in 1934. Her greatest success was *Grand Slam*, a radio quiz show she developed and starred on for CBS from 1943 to 1953. She died in 1980. Francis's WSM programs were a launching pad of sorts for her, and he was proud of her association with his orchestra.[1]

PHIL HARRIS

Among the pros playing for Craig on his first Vanderbilt dance job in 1923 was a teenage drummer named Phil ("Wonga") Harris, who had honed his skills by playing in his father's downtown Knickerbocker Theater orchestra. Harris, a Hume-Fogg High School graduate, left Nashville within weeks of agreeing to be Craig's drummer for Hawaii and a very productive life in music, radio, and film.

He co-led the Lofner-Harris band in the late twenties and early thirties. After taking over the band, he, like Francis, was a hotel orchestra leader. His hotels were, however, more prestigious, the Coconut Grove in Los Angeles and the Waldorf-Astoria in New York. His peers considered his orchestra quite good. He achieved big name recognition through his role on the Jack Benny show as a wisecracking bandleader. After leaving the Benny show in 1946, he had his own show with his wife, Alice Faye. Most of his hit recordings were novelty numbers, especially his drawling of "That's What I

Craig with Harris and Alice Faye.
(Courtesy of Donia Craig Dickerson)

Like about the South." When "Near You" was hot in 1947, Harris's "Smoke! Smoke! Smoke! (That Cigarette)" got as high as number eight on *Billboard*'s Honor Roll. It must have seemed like old times back in Nashville. Harris was in thirteen films. His career was resuscitated in 1967 with his voice role as Baboo the Bear in Disney's *Jungle Book*.

Harris died in 1995. Like many, this graduate's time with Francis was brief. The proper Francis considered Harris a tad loose. The happy, frog-voiced Harris loved girls and produced the first genuine wolf whistle Francis had ever heard.[2]

JAMES (JIMMY) MELTON

No Francis Craig musician had so eclectic a career as James Melton. Born in Moultrie, Georgia, and raised in Ocala, Florida, Melton was a nineteen-year-old-University of Georgia undergraduate in 1923 when Francis Craig played for the junior prom. He approached Francis about a job in his band as a reed man. Francis had no such need but wondered if the curly-headed youngster could sing. Melton auditioned for him by singing "Deep in My Heart." One of Francis's strong points was always his ability to recognize talent. He found a spot for the tenor/saxophonist.

While in Nashville, Melton attended Vanderbilt for one semester, taking mainly languages and racking up the same kind of academic record as his boss's. More important to his career, for three years he studied voice under Gaetano Salvatore de Luca at Ward-Belmont College. He made such excellent progress that he did a southern concert tour, beginning in Ocala, in spring 1926. All the while, he continued to play in Craig's hot orchestra. His saxophone was prominent in the 1925 recordings of "Marble Halls" and "That Florida Low-Down" (see discography).

Craig and Melton became lifelong friends. The sax player/boy singer was handsome, knew it, and cut a wide swath through the Nashville social scene. Melton left for New York in 1927 and the really big show. Craig took a vacation and accompanied Jimmy to the big city to aid in landing a job.

Gaetano de Luca (in white suit, center front) and Jimmy Melton (top row, left) with Ward-Belmont class. (Courtesy of Margo Melton Nutt)

After repeatedly being refused an audition, Melton forced himself on the famous music entrepreneur/producer Samuel Lionel ("Roxy") Rothafel by loudly singing a song in his outer office. Francis accompanied Jimmy during the audition resulting from the aspirant's bravado. Roxy was impressed enough to give him a contract for $250 a week to sing on *Roxy and His Gang,* a variety show that dominated Monday nights on the NBC blue network throughout the late twenties and early thirties.

Melton made four movies, sang with the famous Reveler's Quartet, and was popular in radio through the 1940s. Weathering the initial panning of his work in the early thirties by tough New York critics, he realized the ultimate goal of Sr. de Luca's training in opera. He sang with numerous companies from 1938 and debuted with the Metropolitan Opera in 1942. His best roles were as Tamino in *The Magic Flute* and Pinkerton in *Madame Butterfly.*

Nashville News

A Weekly Publication Devote and Features of General In orts

Vol VII, No. 26—8 Pages   THURSDAY, MAY 8, 1941 SEE,

NASHVILLE PERSONALITIES

Melton in Nashville News.

Francis and his Vanderbilt fraternity brother, Dr. C. Royal ("Tot") McCullough, attended Melton's 1929 wedding in Akron, Ohio. The young men could not afford to take their wives. The bride had met Melton at a performance at the Seiberling (rubber) estate, and some of the wedding party, including Craig, stayed there. Francis derived pleasure over the years from frequently re-telling the anecdote about an Akron cabby who wondered if he and McCullough should be taken to the servant's entrance, only to see them effusively welcomed by the Seiberling butler. All this seemed like real high cotton to the southern boys. Francis enjoyed the amenities of life among the very rich, including a continental breakfast of tea and cinnamon toast. He played for the Seiberlings on the mansion organ and served as a groomsman in Jimmy Melton's wedding ceremony.

Despite his brief time at the school, Melton made numerous appearances at Vanderbilt. Nearly always he referred to his friendship with Francis and the fortuitous direction his life took after signing on with the maestro. Nashville and Francis Craig were also very proud of Melton, who died in 1961.[3]

KENNY SARGENT

Born in Centralia, Illinois, in 1906, Sargent supposedly succeeded Melton as the orchestra's boy singer. Authors Paul J. Broome and Clay Tucker thought Francis must have hired Sargent, also a competent saxophonist, specially for the 1925 Atlanta recording sessions. He was supposedly with other organizations until 1930. Sargent was definitely with Francis Craig in 1930–1931, when he left to go with Glen Gray's Casa Loma Orchestra, an important unit in the history of swing music. He stayed with them for over ten years. The handsome saxophonist was a popular vocalist and had several hits with Gray. He left the band for Memphis in 1943, where he briefly led a band. He closed out his career as a disk jockey in Dallas, dying in 1969.

Like several others, Sargent was with Francis only transiently and apparently gave the bandleader no great credit for his success. Francis called Sargent "the Frank Sinatra of the 30s."[4]

SNOOKY LANDMAN/LANSON

Roy Landman[5] was born in Memphis in 1914. Based on a
song he sang at age two (he started young), his mother
gave him the nickname "Snooky." Educated in Memphis
parochial schools, he was early noted for his athletic and
singing abilities. He sang in St. Patrick's Church choir as a
youngster. Francis supposedly discovered him when some pals
pushed him forward to sing with the band at a Memphis prom
in 1933 or 1934. He joined the orchestra as boy singer in 1935,
instituting a love-hate relationship with his employer, whose
temperament and background were so different from his.

Francis and Landman needed each other but never came
close to getting along. Francis recognized a talented vocalist
with a smooth stage presence. Landman, who sprang from a
poor family, recognized a job with a well-known orchestra. He
was a fun-loving, hard-drinking, irresponsible guy. The bandleader was none of those. In addition to personality
differences, some of Landman's antipathy arose from Francis's
alleged parsimony. Besides being a nonunion singer who made
less than the other performers, Landman felt Francis never
gave him a fair financial shake.

Over the years, the crooner told myriad stories about his first
music boss. Being paid twenty-five dollars per week, Landman
claimed that Francis once did not pay him on the last week of a
five-week month because his salary was really one hundred
dollars per month, which he had already received. Snooky
participated in a fifteen-minute afternoon program at WSM for
weeks before he learned that Francis was getting paid a few bucks
for the show and he was not receiving a dime. Francis supposedly
rationalized that Landman's weekly salary covered that.

Landman found numerous ways, some petty, to gain
revenge for perceived injustice. Because the boy singer had no
instrument, he was responsible for moving the band's sound
system. After lugging the heavy system up a couple of stories in
an Atlanta hotel and getting increasingly angry about the division of labor, Landman dropped the equipment down the
stairwell. The replacement system was a lighter one. He would

sometimes aggravate Francis by reading a newspaper at side stage while waiting for his vocal. Because a lunch table was usually reserved for National Life executives at the Hermitage, Landman circulated a rumor that the company owned a piece of the hotel, implying that Francis was getting yet another break from his family. Landman once said his boss had fired him twice and he had quit thrice, making him one ahead in the contest of wills. It was only economic exigencies that kept the two together most of the time until the War.

In 1941, Landman went with the Ray Noble Orchestra and became Snooky Lanson. Noble thought his given name "sounded too Jewish." From 1942, he was with Ted Weems in the military. After the War, Lanson was back in Nashville with WSM doing his own show, singing with Beasley Smith on his

The Francis Craig Orchestra with Snooky Landman (later Lanson) on the left. (From P. J. Broome and Clay Tucker, The Other Music City, *1990)*

Sunday Down South network show, and singing dances with
Owen Bradley. Apparently he and Francis Craig had had
enough of each other.

After a successful 1949 recording of Smith's "Lucky Old Sun"
in the Ryman Auditorium, Lanson was recommended as a
replacement for Frank Sinatra on "Your Hit Parade." He was
notified of this while on vacation with his family in Florida. Never
overwhelmed with ambition, he declined the opportunity—until
he was told the starting salary was $750 per week. Without
rehearsal, he did his first live show in summer 1950. He stayed
until 1957, making a lot of money and spending most of it.
During that time, the careers of Craig graduates coincidentally
crossed when he did a summer replacement television show for
Dinah Shore. Lanson played New York clubs until 1962, when he
moved to Atlanta for a couple of years of television. He was fired
from that job, apparently because of alcoholism, a family trait.

Though refraining from taking his favorite Seagram's VO
before lunch, Lanson never stayed on the wagon the rest of his
life. When sober, he was a pleasant, good man graced with loyal
fans, many of whom he earned on radio spots on WAMB after
his return to Nashville in 1968. Carefree in his case also
connoted careless. He had no clue about money management,
never even had a checkbook. Neither could he ever turn down
a request for money. He died in 1990 from lung cancer. His
family realized nothing of the big money he earned during his
best career years on *Your Hit Parade*.[6]

Snooky Lanson and Francis Craig were as different as Goell
and Craig. The wonder is that the Methodist aristocrat related
well enough to them for long enough to make a little music
history. He must have recognized something worthwhile in each.

PEE WEE MARQUETTE

Perhaps the most memorable performer to Francis Craig fans
between the mid-thirties and the mid-forties was Pee Wee
Marquette. Few knew and no one used his last name. In hiring
him in 1934, Francis cleverly placed some dynamism in front of the

orchestra that he had never pretended to provide. Pee Wee was a sixteen-year-old black midget, who supposedly approached Francis at the Hermitage Hotel. He had been a mascot for the University of Alabama football team and worked as a page in a Montgomery hotel. Because of his age, the Tennessee legislature had to waive his minority status in order to have him work for Craig. He was three feet nine inches tall and said to weigh anywhere from forty-five to ninety pounds (probably closer to the latter). His skills included tap dancing, ukulele strumming, imitations, and singing songs with double entendres ("Shine," "Me and My Shadow"). His performance role could best be classified as a "personality." Dressed as a bellhop, reminiscent of Phillip Morris's "Johnny," he provided light humor in an era when blacks were often valued as much for their ostensibly exotic

Francis Craig and Pee Wee Marquette broadcast nationally. (From Blair School of Music display)

nature as their talent—a la Stepin Fetchit or Amos 'n' Andy.

Pee Wee was adored in Nashville, but his charm was not just a southern phenomenon. When Francis took him on a holiday trip, the bandleader was asked by bandleader Kay Kyser to perform at the Blackhawk Restaurant in Chicago. Francis deferred to his half-pint companion, who proceeded to bring the house down with his rendition of "Minnie the Moocher." A Nashville paper suggested this performance was the obverse of General Sherman's march through Georgia.

As with the Francis Craig orchestra, no nickname or descriptive phrase was ever consistently attached to him. Publicity spots

FRANCIS CRAIC
and His Mascot
" PEE WEE "

Postcard with Pee Wee. (Courtesy of Ridley Wills II)

and newspaper squibs variously called him "ninety pounds of dynamite," "the diminutive darky," "Dixie dynamite," "that cunning rascal," and Francis Craig's "chocolate drop mascot." Pee Wee performed with gusto and would use the experience to move on in the entertainment world. Francis had considerable trouble preventing other band-leaders from hiring Pee Wee away from him. Sometime during World War II, he hired an agent for Pee Wee, who cut out for the Big Apple. In New York, he worked as a greeter (some claimed master of ceremonies) at the Zanzibar and Birdland night clubs. Clint Garvin fondly recalled some Harlem club-hopping with Pee Wee, who would always be absent when the bill arrived.

No one knows what Pee Wee's perception of his role with Francis Craig was. Race was an issue. Snooky Landman felt it demeaning to appear as an equal with the black midget on stage. Francis solved that problem by having them on opposite ends. When Francis was occasionally late for a set at the Hermitage, the boys would strike up a racist number, after which Pee Wee would threaten to "tell Mr. Craig" on them. Travel arrangements on the road were sometimes difficult. When Pee Wee visited the Craigs for Sunday dinner, he sat at a separate, small table in order not to insult their maid by having her serve another colored person at the dining table. When Francis visited the Club Zanzibar where Pee Wee was working, the little fellow introduced his former boss as being from the Midwest, thereby politely avoiding the stigma attached to southern origin.

Most of the band's musicians came to respect Pee Wee as a smart, somewhat talented, opportunistic man. He made great friends among the young society set, at whose birthday parties he frequently entertained. Over the years, he maintained contact with several of them. He left Nashville with many friends, having reaped the benefits of Francis Craig's employment and encouragement.[7]

DINAH SHORE

Dinah (née Frances, Fanny, or Fannye Rose) Shore came rocketing out of Nashville in the early 1940s to become one of the most important entertainers of the latter half of her century. In Nashville her name has always been associated with Francis Craig's orchestra, whatever influence he had on her career. Her family had moved to Nashville from rural Winchester, Tennessee, when she was six years old. In the early 1930s, the teen-aged Fannye lived at 3745 Whitland Avenue, across the street and one-half block east of Francis Craig. Like Phil Harris, she attended Hume-Fogg High School. In another of her romantic, probably fanciful, accounts, Bowen Ingram told of the young lady seeking Francis's help as she began her career in entertainment when she was a freshman at Vanderbilt in 1934. Recognizing her seriousness, Francis supposedly obtained an audition for her at WSM. Her first show at WSM was a twice-weekly, fifteen-minute bit called "Rhythm and Romance," for which she was paid five to ten dollars a pop. There was also a Friday night prefootball weekend shindig called "Fanny Rose Shore, Our Little Cheerleader of Song." She worked with Francis both at the station and occasionally at the Hermitage but did not go on the road with him.

Full of spunk, Dinah set out for New York on graduation from Vanderbilt in 1938. After failing to catch on with numerous major bands, she recorded with Xavier Cugat and sang on radio. She joined Eddie Cantor's radio show in 1940 and became a star. She made some forgettable movies, had nine gold records, and worked hard entertaining U.S. troops in the

Dinah on piano in front of Craig orchestra. (From Vanderbilt Alumnus, *spring 1982)*

War. Ever resourceful and ambitious, she had a huge television career. Her top-rated variety show, *The Dinah Shore Chevy Show,* ran from 1956–1963. She followed that with several talk shows in the seventies and eighties. In all, she won eight Emmy Awards. She died in February 1994.

Dinah Shore was well loved in Nashville. Though some of the musicians called her the "sweetheart of the YMHA" (Young Men's Hebrew Association), her religious faith was no factor on the Vanderbilt campus, where she was a popular student leader. She was recalled as a tomboy, a good sport, "just a great girl." Marj Cooney remembered her driving downtown in her convertible filled with football players. While recognizing her intelligence and ambition, WSM personnel adored her.

Discerning Nashville musicians did not think much of her voice. She occasionally had trouble with the pitch and was not as talented as Kitty Kallen, another Francis Craig vocalist. Her voice improved with work, but her warm personality, the key to her show business success, shone through regardless of the product of her pipes.

Nashville would clearly never contain Dinah. She remained loyal to the city and Vanderbilt. Greer Ricketson recalled entering a concert she was giving for GIs in Paris during World War II. In her unaffected fashion, Dinah interrupted the show and asked him and his pal to come backstage afterwards.

Though Dinah spent only a short professional time with Francis, she is the most famous entertainer ever lumped into the category of his graduates. He helped her get started but was not her prime sponsor or mentor. Dinah never publicly recognized any such aid. She may have believed, probably correctly, that she was her own creation.[8]

KITTY KALLEN

Kitty Kallen (a stage name) was born in Philadelphia in 1922, the daughter of Jewish parents, a Russian immigrant mother and a barber father. She began winning local talent shows as a songbird at age seven. Her big break was appearing on the *Horn & Hardart Children's Hour* programs on station WCAU. Her relationship with her father was strained, and she left home at age sixteen to join Jack Teagarden's band.

Jack Teagarden formed a wonderful big band in 1939. Among its employees was Clint Garvin, apparently on his way to the big time from Francis's band. Teagarden was the greatest jazz trombonist of all time. He was also an alcoholic with no business sense. Within a year, the Teagarden big band had failed. This occurred in part because Teagarden paid his players too much. Clint Garvin reported being paid ninety dollars per week. Glenn Miller at the time was paying sixty-five, about what Clint was getting back in Nashville with Francis. After the breakup of Teagarden's band, Clint headed back south to rejoin Francis. His new flame, Kallen, came to Nashville in 1940 to work with WSM and Francis Craig.

Francis Craig and Kitty Kallen, in a pose reminiscent of a later, similar publicity photo of Harry Truman and Lauren Bacall. (From Blair School of Music display)

In early 1941, Clint Garvin supposedly married Kitty Kallen in Franklin, Kentucky. That union could not be found in the county marriage register. Kallen claimed the marriage was "annulled" because she was underage. (Clint had also neglected to tell her he had previously enjoyed marital bliss.) Her whole Nashville experience seemed to have been unpleasant. In her first exposure to the South, she felt a lot of anti-Semitism. She claimed to have clobbered a piano player in a bar one night when, after a heated argument, he asserted one couldn't argue with "a nigger or a Jew." Garvin somehow doubted this occurred, although he remembered a nightclub with a sign saying "No Jews Allowed." Jud Collins remembered Kitty, on a grim winter day while looking out an upstairs window at WSM, vehemently and profanely expressing her distaste for Nashville.

Well, she was not around very long. After less than a year, she left for the West Coast. In liner notes for her 1992 compact disc, *The Kitty Kallen Story*, Kallen completely skipped over her Nashville experience, saying she went directly from the dissolution of Teagarden's big band to the Coast. She contradicted herself later in the narrative by saying, "I sang with Francis Craig in Nashville on WSM."

Kallen was sure she could do better than Nashville; she was right. She became quite successful in California. Once more, Francis Craig alumni found each other. Kallen roomed with Dinah Shore for some time in Los Angeles. She hit it big with Jimmy Dorsey, having records listed from one through four on the *Billboard* chart in 1943 and 1944. She later worked with Artie Shaw and Harry James, her favorite bandleader. Her biggest hit, "Little Things Mean a Lot," was number one in 1954. Her last chart single, "My Coloring Book," was recorded in 1962.

Kitty Kallen had a superb voice, a pleasing stage presence, and an important career. Most musicians thought she had more talent than Dinah Shore. Francis Craig and Nashville only briefly enjoyed her work. It was regrettable she felt so alien to the place, an attitude opposite that of the relaxed, convivial Dinah. Nashville and the South were not noted for their racial and ethnic tolerance in 1940. Still, most everyone got along, and prejudice was not as big a problem in the entertainment business as in the general society. The large cultural chip on Kitty Kallen's pretty shoulder may have had something to do with her misery.[9]

THE BOYS IN THE BAND

Numerous Francis Craig instrumentalists and vocalists played in a higher league after their time with Nashville's best orchestra. Most moved between bands, depending on opportunity, but while in Nashville were more often with Francis because he was so reliably busy.

Malcom Crain, a Dickson native like Francis, played trumpet with him until 1927, when he joined the Doc Ross band in Texas. Included in that talented group was a young Jack Teagarden. Crain returned to Francis's orchestra during most of the thirties but toured and recorded with Artie Shaw and Woody Herman late in the decade.

Clint Garvin ran away from Castle Heights Military Academy at age seventeen to join Beasley Smith on the road. He was mostly with Francis Craig from 1931 to 1939. His good reed work landed him a job on Jack Teagarden's big, excellent band until it imploded. He returned to work with a smaller Teagarden band in 1941. In the early fifties, he played several months with Ziggy Elman and His Orchestra.

The two Johnston boys were Nashville East High graduates who cut a vocal swath through Nashville. The elder, Bob sang only occasionally with Francis. Adopting the stage name Bob Johnstone, he was with Paul Whiteman and Shep Fields in New York during the early forties. After returning to Nashville, he sang mostly with Beasley Smith's WSM orchestra. The younger Johnston, Howard, using the stage name Gene Howard, sang more with Francis during the early forties. He used to confuse Francis by singing songs correctly. The leader had only heard them sung by Snooky Lanson, who could not read music and had sung the tunes incorrectly. Howard later sang with Bob Chester and Stan Kenton.[10]

Several Francis Craig players stayed in Nashville and had bands of their own. These included Red McEwen, Jimmy Gallagher, John Gordy, and Cecil Bailey. When Gordy and the Alabama boys, Newt Richardson and Cecil Bailey, joined the WSM orchestra after the War, Francis took it personally. He should have recognized that despite years of work with the Southern Maestro, their economic allegiance was to themselves, and Francis Craig's star was fading when they moved.

There's just one place for me, NEAR YOU.

finale

Final Movement

Library and archival staff in Francis Craig's hometown, the Athens of the South, cordially provided direction as well as material and references. I particularly thank Ronnie Pugh and John Rumble of the Country Music Foundation Library and Media Center, Cathy Smith of the Special Collections Section of the Jean and Alexander Heard (Vanderbilt) Library, Shirley Watts of the (Vanderbilt) Blair School of Music Library, Carol Kaplan and Mary Glenn Hearne of the Nashville Room of the Public Library of Nashville and Davidson County, and Jenella Olker of the Tennessee State Library and Archives.

Much information came from musicians, many of whom worked with Francis Craig—the girls and boys in the band. They were candid and pleasant, apparently enjoying talking about the old days. Though there were others, I extend a special literary fanfare to Harold Bradley, Mary Cortner (Ragland), Christine Johnson (Smith), Beverly LeCroy, Paul Lenk, Will T. Malone, Ann Parman (Vaughn), and Walt Summers. My best source and telephone buddy, Clint Garvin, died in February 1999. Clint was professionally emoting into his beloved saxophone until he just ran out of breath. Among gifted and helpful musicians of a later generation were Beegie Adair, Layng Martine, and Bob McDill. These nice people wanted to learn about Francis Craig as they taught me so much.

Francis Craig's family were receptive and generous. They never attempted to influence my research direction or conclusions. I thank his cousins of various remove—C. A. Craig II, Douglas Henry, Elizabeth Proctor, and Margaret Ann Robinson.

Craig's immediate family was a joy to work with. His widow, Elizabeth Lancaster, is a charming, honest lady. I appreciated the privilege of getting to know her. Mr. and Mrs. Lane Abernathy were unhesitatingly supportive. Tragically, Celeste Craig Abernathy died in August 1998. Donia Craig Dickerson provided major materials, including several illustrations and her scrapbook about her father, a copy of which is in the Craig Papers in the Special Collections Section at Vanderbilt. More importantly, Donia, with her energetic interest in the project, was always available. Francis Craig must have been a very good man to have earned the love of Elizabeth, Celeste, and Donia.

Apropos of nothing in the book, the author herewith takes literary license to end with some humor by one of Nashville's greatest raconteurs and jokesters. At a winter 1999 Coffee House Club meeting, I had a conversation with Mr. Fred Russell, longtime, nationally recognized Nashville Banner sportswriter. Fred, now well over ninety years old, had been in ill health, was recovering, but was still a tad less forthright than his friends were accustomed to. I reminded him I was writing a book about Francis Craig. Without hesitancy and with a quiet, slightly stammering voice, he immediately quipped, "Craig? Why he wrote the song about that Indian guy, Neh-ru."

Nuff said! Thanks for the memories, Fred. A merry heart doeth good like a medicine (Prov. 17:22).

Appendix A

DISCOGRAPHY[1]

Title	Recording/Release Date	Label
Marble Halls/Steady Roll Blues	29 September 1925/———	Columbia 567-D
Hard-to-Get Gertie/Do You Believe in Dreams?[2]	April 1926/———	Columbia 709-D
That Florida Low-Down/Moonlight in Mandalay	22 April 1926/———	Columbia 1266-D
Forgiveness/Mighty Lak' a Rose	29 September 1925/———	Columbia 495-D
Ting-a-ling/In the Middle of the Night	21 April 1926/———	Columbia 649-D
All Day Long/Dream River	16 April 1928/———	Columbia 1440-D
Red Rose/Coon-Tail	16 April 1928/———	Columbia 1544-D
Red Rose/Near You	20 February 1947/———	Bullet 1001
Beg Your Pardon/Looking for a Sweetheart	unknown	Bullet 1012
Foolin'/Do Me a Favor, Will You?	unknown	Bullet 1013
I Still Get a Thrill/Disallusioned [sic]	unknown	Bullet 1040
Tennessee Tango/I Thought I Was Dreaming	31 January 1949/———	MGM 10378
Away from You/Forgiveness	31 January 1949/———	MGM 10468

Title	Recording/ Release Date	Label
The Whole Year 'Round/ My Tears Are Still Falling for You	5 August 1949/———	MGM 10558
Don't Make Me Sorry/ It Was Easter, I Remember	5 August 1949/ 19 January 1950	MGM 10662
For the First Time/Play Them Bones	17 December 1951/ 4 February 1952	Decca 27937
Near You/Stars and Stripes Medley	3 March 1952/ 28 April 1952	Decca 28089
S.O.S. Baby/Too Much Sugar for a Dime	17 December 1951, 3 January 1952/ 16 August 1954	Decca 29143
In the Shade of the Moonlight/If You Care At All	———/24 June 1955	DOT 45-15400
Near You/Beg Your Pardon	———/1980	MCA P-2710

Appendix B

CATALOGUE

Song	Associated Parties	Publisher	Date
A Broken Heart Must Cry		Bregman Vocco & Conn, Inc.	1953
Away from You		Supreme Music Corp.	n.d.
Beg Your Pardon	Beasley Smith	Robbins Music Corp.	1947
Do Me a Favor, Will You?	Beasley Smith	Milene Music, Inc./Edwin H. Morris & Co.	1948
Don't Make Me Sorry	Beasley Smith	Shapiro Bernstein & Co./Milene Music, Inc.	1949
Foolin'	Jack Clifford Charles Farrow	Jay-Dee Music Corp.	1937
Forgiveness		Robbins Music Corp.	1949
Hot Biscuits	Jack Hoffman Gilbert Mills	Arrow Music Co.	n.d.
I Thought I Was Dreaming	Harry A. Carlson Tommy Nolan	Miller Music Corp.	1937
If You Care At All[1]	Kermit Goell	unknown	n.d.
I'll Trade Ya Me for You	Fred Rose	unknown	n.d.
In My Dreams	Sunny Clapp	Anne Rachel Music Corp.	1950
In the Shade of the Moonlight[2]	Kermit Goell	unknown	n.d.
It Hurts Me More Than, etc.	Ellis Seger	Miller Music Corp.	1948
It Was Easter, I Remember		Bregman Vocco & Conn, Inc.	n.d.

155

Song	Associated Parties	Publisher	Date
Learning	Billy Moll	Milene Music, Inc.	1953
Lost Motion	Clint Garvin	Joe Davis, Inc.	1938
My Tears Are Still Falling for You		Anne Rachel Music Corp.	1949
Nashville Banner March		*Nashville Banner* Publishing Co.	1951
Near You	Kermit Goell	Supreme Music Corp.	1947
Play Them Bones	Beasley Smith	Northern Music Corp.	1952
Put All Your Love in a Cookie Jar	George Morgan	Alamo Music, Inc./ Anne Rachel Music, Inc.	1949
Red Rose		Forster Music Publisher, Inc.	1937
Sally Please Don't Dilly Dal	Graydon J. Hall Wallace Fowler	MCA, Inc.	n.d.
She's a Bad Little Girl		Milene Music, Inc.	1950
Silver Wings		unknown	n.d.
Sometimes I Wonder	Will Collins Russ David	Edwin H. Morris & Co., Inc.	1945
Tennessee Tango	Beasley Smith	Robbins Music Corp.	n.d.
The Whole Year 'Round	Beasley Smith	Bristol Music Corp.	1949
Too Much Sugar for a Dime	Bealey Smith	Anne Rachel Music, Inc.	1954
When Vandy Starts to Fight		Edwin H. Morris & Co., Inc.	1941
When Your Lips Touch Mine	Beasley Smith	Milene Music, Inc.	1955
Yearning		Forster Music Publisher	n.d.
You	Sunny Clapp	unknown	n.d.

Notes

Prelude

1. I enjoyed an inconspicuous back-row experience in the *a capella* choir at Vanderbilt.

2. Paul J. Broome and Clay Tucker, *The Other Music City: The Bands and Jazz Musicians of Nashville,1920 to 1970* (Nashville: American Press Print, 1990), (hereinafter cited as Broome and Tucker, *The Other Music City*). The stark tripartite geographical division of Tennessee resulted in three distinct cultures. Citizens are sometimes more proud of and attuned to their so-called Grand Division than they are to the state as a whole.

3. Aaron Shelton, telephone interview by author, New Johnsonville, Tenn., 23 March 1998.

4. Powell Stamper, *The National Life Story* (New York: Appleton-Century-Crofts, 1968, 29–42 (hereinafter cited as Stamper, *National Life*).

Chapter One: Andante Ma Con Brio

1. Bowen Ingram, "The Story of Francis Craig" (Lebanon, Tennessee, c. 1950), 1 (hereinafter cited as Ingram MSS). Bowen Ingram was the *nom de plume* of Mrs. Daniel (Mildred Prewitt) Ingram. She apparently worked on this manuscript with Francis Craig. It was found in some papers of Donia Craig Dickerson. Appended to it was a note to Francis from Mrs. Ingram asking his review, apparently in anticipation of its publication. The piece has many errors, and it is unclear which of the recorded anecdotes came from Francis or the author's imagination. I have not referred to it for critical information. See Clara Heironymous, "Bowen Ingram: A Remembrance," *Nashville Tennessean*, 16 March 1980, 11-F (hereinafter cited as *NT*).

2. "Two Survivors from Galveston Estimate the Loss of Life There at Two Thousand," *Nashville American*, 10 September 1900, 1 (hereinafter cited as *NA*); "William M'Kinley's Letter of Acceptance," *NA*, 1; "Democratic Ticket," *NA*, 4; "Appalling Calamity on Southern Coast," *Nashville Banner*, 10 September 1900, 1, 8 (hereinafter cited as *NB*); "Mr. M'Kinley's Letter of Acceptance Well Received in Chicago," *NB*, 1, 8; *Twelfth Census of the United States, 1900*, vol. 1 (Washington: United States Census Office, 1901), xviii (hereinafter cited as *Twelfth Census*). A comprehensive pictorial depiction of life at the turn of the twentieth century was provided by the television production, David Grubin and Judy

Crichton, *America 1900*, Corporation for Public Broadcasting, 1998.

3. *Twelfth Census*, 39; John Trotwood Moore and Austin P. Foster, *Tennessee, The Volunteer State, 1760–1923* (Nashville: S. J. Clarke Publishing Company, 1923), 583–590; Stanley J. Folmsbee, Robert E. Corlew, and Enoch L. Mitchell, *Tennessee: A Short History* (Knoxville: The University of Tennessee Press, 1972), 430–433 (hereinafter cited as Corlew and Mitchell, *Tennessee: A Short History*).

4. *Twelfth Census*, 39, 476, 556; Jill Knight Garrett, *Dickson County Handbook* (Southern Historical Press, Inc., 1984), 329; Robert Ewing Corlew, *A History of Dickson County Tennessee* (The Tennessee Historical Commission and The Dickson County Historical Society, 1956), 132; *The Home Enterprise* (Dickson, Tennessee), 9 June 1899, 1; Robert W. Clement, "From Mile Post 42 . . . To City of Dickson 1980," *Dickson Free Press*, 9 January 1980 and 13 February 1980.

5. Irving Sablosky, *American Music* (Chicago: University of Chicago Press, 1969), 112–114 (hereinafter cited as Sablosky, *American Music*); Gilbert Chase, "The Rise of Ragtime," chap. 23 in *America's Music from Pilgrims to the Present*, 3d ed. (Urbana: University of Illinois Press, 1987), 413–428 (hereinafter cited as Chase, *America's Music*).

6. Sablosky, *American Music*, 116–122; Chase, *America's Music*, 506.

7. Hazel Meyer, *The Gold in Tin Pan Alley* (Philadelphia: J. B. Lippincott Company, 1958), 30–43 (hereinafter cited as Meyer, *Tin Pan Alley*); Roger Kinkle, *The Complete Encyclopedia of Popular Music and Jazz, 1900–1950*, 4 vols. (New Rochelle, N.Y.: Arlington House, 1974), xxix–xxx (hereinafter cited as Kinkle, *Popular Music and Jazz*); Chase, *America's Music*, 336–339.

8. Russell Sanjek and David Sanjek, *American Popular Music Business in the 20th Century* (New York: Oxford University Press, 1991), vii-viii, 3–4 (hereinafter cited as Sanjek and Sanjek, *American Popular Music*).

9. Fannie Craig died 13 September 1947, age eighty-five. She is buried in Nashville's Mt. Olivet Cemetery alongside her husband.

10. Celeste Craig Abernathy provided genealogical information on Fannie Frost. Rev. Von W. Unruh of the Tennessee Conference (Methodist) Commission on Archives and History provided information on Robert James Craig's life and career. Emory and Henry College provided me a copy of

Craig's award-winning speech there. Information on his year at Vanderbilt is in a file on him at the Vanderbilt Divinity School alumni office.

11. Mabel Pittard, *Rutherford County*, Tennessee County History Series (Memphis: Memphis State University Press, 1985), 49–50.

12. Father Craig died March 7, 1937 in Deland, Florida. Though some of his relatives thought his sermons incredibly boring, many thought he had a sense of humor, probably much more so than his son, Francis. Robert Craig was much honored in the Methodist Church. Two churches in Davidson County, Craig Memorial Church and Craig Memorial Chapel, were named for him. He is buried in Nashville's Mt. Olivet Cemetery. See "Rev. R. J. Craig, Veteran Minister, Dies in Florida," *NB*, 8 March 37, 1911.

13. Ingram MSS, 2–9; Francis Craig Papers, Special Collections Section, Vanderbilt University Library (hereinafter cited as Craig Papers). A program for one of Craig's recitals shows compositions by, among others, Mozart, Paderewski, Godard, and Liszt.

14. Address by Lane Abernathy (Francis Craig's son-in-law) at R. J. Craig family reunion, Florida, summer 1993; Elizabeth Gewin Craig Lancaster (Francis Craig's widow), interview by author, Sewanee, Tenn., 28 March 1998; Mary Elizabeth Black, telephone interview by author, Tallahassee, Fla., 9 June 1998; Elizabeth Wilkes Romine, "In the Rockies," unknown Pulaski, Tenn., newspaper, 1930. Craig Papers. Francis Craig called himself a "PK."

15. Walter Durham thought the concert was held in a more sedate setting, Howard College adjacent to the Methodist parsonage. See Walter Durham, *A History of the First United Methodist Church, Gallatin, Tennessee* (Gallatin: n.p., 1984), 8; Lancaster, interview, 28 March 1998; Ingram MSS, 9–12; Virginia Bivin, "I Remember . . .," *NB*, 27 August 1955, 14 (hereinafter cited as Bivin, "I Remember."

16. Ridley Wills II, "The Old Boys' Schools of Middle Tennessee," *Tennessee Historical Quarterly* (spring 1997): 56, 67; *NB*, "Rites held for retired Gen. Craig," 26 January 1982, C-7; Francis Craig, Vanderbilt University transcript, courtesy of University Registrar; Lancaster, interview, Sewanee, Tenn., 31 January 1998. The Massey School graduation program of Craig's class of twenty-three students is in the Craig Papers of Elizabeth Gewin Craig Lancaster.

17. Craig Papers; Ingram MSS, 13. Francis's twin brothers became career officers after World War I.

18. Francis Craig, WSM radio interview by Jo Sherman, 1962.

19. Though generally not recognized, industrial-life policies are still afoot in the land. American General Life and Accident, the company which bought NLT (later name of National Life), was servicing 149.2 million policy dollars in Florida in 1998. See Chad Terhune, "State Regulators Examine Industrial-Life Insurance," *Wall Street Journal*, 21 October 1998, S1, S4.

20. Stamper, *National Life*, chaps. 3, 4; Don H. Doyle, *Nashville in the New South 1880–1930* (Knoxville: The University of Tennessee Press, 1985), 56–58 (hereinafter cited as Doyle, *Nashville in the New South*); Lancaster, interview, 28 March 1998. As Doyle notes, the current sources about National Life are the company newspaper, various speeches, and Stamper's salutary company history.

21. *Alumni Directory*, vol. 1 (Nashville: Vanderbilt University Alumni Association, 1923), 131 (hereinafter cited as Vanderbilt *Alumni Directory*).

22. Paul K. Conkin, "Nuts and Bolts," in *Gone with the Ivy: A Biography of Vanderbilt University* (Knoxville: The University of Tennessee Press, 1985), 225–258 (hereinafter cited as Conkin, *Gone with the Ivy*).

23. Edwin Mims, "The Ten Years' War," in *Chancellor Kirkland of Vanderbilt* (Nashville: Vanderbilt University Press, 1940), 160–196.

24. Conkin, *Gone with the Ivy*, 231; Robert A. McGaw, *A Brief History of Vanderbilt University* (Nashville: Vanderbilt University Press, 1973), 20–21, 27; Edwin Mims, *History of Vanderbilt University* (Nashville: Vanderbilt University Press, 1946), 325.

25. Ingram MSS, 13; "University Records," Vanderbilt University catalog, 1918–1920, 44. There is a check signed by Francis in the amount of fifteen dollars for his 1922 tuition in the Craig Papers. R. J.'s children were probably given some ministerial relief by the recently Methodist university.

26. "Fugitives and Agrarians," in Conkin, *Gone with the Ivy*, 313–346; C. A. Craig II, "Craig Tops Hit Parade with 'Near You,'" *Scroll of Phi Delta Theta* (January 1948); Jay Langhammer, "Phis in Arts and Entertainment," *Scroll* (spring 1997); "Southern Phi a Musical Success," *Scroll* (March 24): 359–360;

"May your future be as successful as your past," congratulatory telegram from Tennessee Alpha to Francis Craig on the occasion of his last NBC broadcast, 4 May 1946, Craig Papers.

27. Ingram MSS, 13, 14; Craig, Vanderbilt transcript. Francis's address beneath the Phi Delta Theta composite in the 1922 *Commodore*, the Vanderbilt yearbook, was Rockford, Ill.

28. Lancaster, interview, 28 March 1998; Craig, Vanderbilt transcript; Ingram MSS, 14; Bivin, "I Remember"; *Commodore*, 1919. Francis, himself, was probably responsible for perpetuating the story about his band's first paying job. Frank Godchaux Jr. was important to Vanderbilt. He was a quarterback on the 1921 football team; see Fred Russell and Benson Maxwell, *Fifty Years of Vanderbilt Football* (Nashville: n.p., 1938), (hereinafter cited as Russell and Maxwell, *Fifty Years of Vanderbilt Football*); Godchaux became one of the outstanding amateur golfers in the South; see Morgan B. Reynolds, *Seventy Years of Belle Meade Country Club, 1901–1971* (Nashville: McQuiddy Printing Co., 1971), (hereinafter cited as Reynolds, *Belle Meade Country Club*). The main building of Vanderbilt Nursing School was named Godchaux Hall in honor of Frank's wife after the family contributed to its renovation in 1971; see Mary Louise Donaldson, *A History of the Vanderbilt School of Nursing* (Nashville: Vanderbilt University Press, 1985), 52.

29. J. A. Simpson and E. S. C. Weiner, *The Oxford English Dictionary*, 2d ed., vol. 8 (Oxford: Clarendon Press, 1989), 52; Chase, *American Music*, 507; Ronald L. Davis, *The Modern Era, 1920–Present*, vol. 3 of *A History of Music in American Life* (Malabar, Fla.: Robert Krieger Publishing Company, 1981), 296–297 (hereinafter cited as Davis, *A History of Music*). The word "jazz" was increasingly used and was frequently seen in the Vanderbilt student newspaper. See *Hustler*, "Vandy Symphony Orchestra Will Out-Jazz Sewanee," 17 November 1921, 1, 4.

30. George T. Simon, *Glenn Miller and His Orchestra* (New York: Thomas Y. Crowell Company, 1974), 31, 33, 36; Craig, "Personality of the Day," WSM radio interview, c. 1938; Lancaster, interview, 31 January 1998. The story of the Kirkland ultimatum is perpetuated in a historical marker in front of Francis's Whitland Avenue Nashville home.

31. Vanderbilt *Alumni Directory*, 131; Mary Elizabeth Black, interview, 9 June 1998; Craig, Vanderbilt transcript; Lancaster, interview, 28 March 1998; Ingram MSS, 14. Vanderbilt could not even decide what class Francis belonged to. An alumni department flier in the Craig Papers lists him in "Who's Who In '22 40 Years Later." He is listed in the same class in John F. Sawyer and Cameron F. Sawyer, "Big Bands Then and Now," *Vanderbilt Alumnus* (spring 1982): 27 (hereinafter cited as Sawyer and Sawyer, "Big Bands"). In "Memories of Music," *Vanderbilt Magazine* (winter 1993): 4, he is called a member of the class of 1923. In a Vanderbilt student newspaper article, he's said to be from the class of 1924, "When Vandy Starts to Fight," *Hustler*, 23 November 1938, 2.

32. Reynolds, *Belle Meade Country Club*; Oscar Cromwell Tidwell Jr., *Belle Meade Park* (Nashville: n.p., 1983), 78–89; Doyle, *Nashville in the New South*, 98.

33. Ingram MSS, 18; Lancaster, interviews, 31 January 1998 and 28 March 1998; Lancaster, telephone interviews, Sewanee, Tenn., 6 July 1998 and 1 October 1998; R. J. Craig, Sparta, Tenn., letter to Francis Craig, Nashville, 17 April 1924, Craig Papers; "Miss Gewin to Wed Mr. Francis Craig," *Birmingham News*, 20 October 1924, 14; "Home Wedding of Miss Gewin And Mr. Craig," *Birmingham Age-Herald*, 21 October 1924, 7; Henry Gewin, telephone interview by author, Mobile, Ala., 14 September 1998. Elizabeth's first cousin, Henry Gewin, was a Founder's Medalist in medicine at Vanderbilt in 1945.

34. Lancaster, telephone interviews, 1 October 1998 and 5 October 1998. Francis Craig had managed to get his orchestra together for a recording session in Atlanta on January 27, 1925. Columbia rejected their recording of "Marble Halls" and "Steady Roll Blues." Brian Rust, *Jazz Records 1897–1942*, vol. 1 (New Rochelle, N. Y.: Arlington House, 1978), 355–356 (hereinafter cited as Rust, *Jazz Records*).

35. This term much loved by the Nashville Chamber of Commerce is usually attributed to a WSM on-air remark by announcer David Cobb in 1950. See John Lomax III, *Nashville Music City USA* (New York: Harry N. Abrams, Inc., 1985), 7 (hereinafter cited as Lomax, *Nashville Music City*).

Chapter Two: Allegretto

1. R. Jackson Wilson and others, "Mass Culture and the 'Jazz Age,'" in *The Pursuit of Liberty: A History of the American*

People, 2d ed. (Wadsworth Publishing Company: Belmont, California, 1990), 833–871 (hereinafter cited as Wilson, *The Pursuit of Liberty*).

2. Sablosky, *American Music*, 147; "Jazz: Tradition and Transformation," in Chase, *America's Music*, 506–524; Kinkle, *Popular Music and Jazz*, xxxii, xxxiii; "The Evolution of Jazz," chap. in Davis, *A History of Music*, 289–324; "Popular Songs," in Davis, *A History of Music*, 325–351.

3. Marirose Arendale, "Tennessee and Woman's Rights," *Tennessee Historical Quarterly* 34 (spring 1980): 62–78; Dewey W. Grantham, "Tennessee and Twentieth-Century Politics," *Tennessee Historical Quarterly* 54 (fall 1995): 214; *Fifteenth Census of the United States, 1930*, vol. 3, pt. 2 (Washington: United States Census Office, 1932), 873 (hereinafter cited as *Fifteenth Census*); Corlew and Mitchell, *Tennessee: A Short History*, 519–520.

4. "Flush Times in War and Peace," in Doyle, *Nashville in the New South*, 183–211; "On the Wall Street of the South," in Doyle, 212–232; Wilson, *The Pursuit of Liberty*, 856; Lancaster, telephone interview, 12 October 1998.

5. Fleming Smith criticized the architectural descriptions. Fleming Smith, conversation with author, Nashville, 3 May 1999; "Hermitage Hotel Will Open Today," *NT*, 17 September 1910, 3; "Hermitage Hotel Informally Opens Doors to Public," *NT*, 18 September 1910, part 2, 1, 3; "Opening of Great Hotel," *NB*, 19 September 1910, 2; "Hotel Hermitage," *Pen and Sunlight Sketches of Nashville*, 76, 77, reprint, Hermitage Hotel folder in Nashville Room, Nashville Public Library; Max York, "The Hermitage: Days of Grandeur," *NT*, 3 July 1977, 1-F, 2-F; Hieronymus, "Nashville Beaux Arts Work Doomed?" *NT*, 14 August 1977, 4-E, 5-E; Hieronymus, "The Hermitage: An Aging Beauty Recovers Status," *NT*, 4 February 1981, 35, 38; Peter Mikelbani, "What the Bellman Knew!" *Nashville Magazine*, September 1986, 66.

6. Charles Hamm, *Yesterdays: Popular Song in America* (New York: W. W. Norton & Company, 1979), 380–381 (hereinafter cited as Hamm, *Yesterdays: Popular Song*).

7. Lancaster, telephone interview, 1 October 1998. Guests at the Hermitage Hotel from the time of Craig's employment there included Al Jolson, Jack Dempsey, Eleanor Roosevelt, Gene Autry, Helen Hays, Bette Davis, Paul

Whiteman, and Al Capone.

8. This listing of schools comes from some publicity materials in the Craig Papers; *Commodore*, 1930, features section.

9. *Marshall-Bruce-Polk Cos.'s Nashville City Directory (1926)*, (Nashville: Marshall-Bruce-Polk); Lancaster, telephone interview, 12 October 1998. Though purchased in 1925, the house was not registered until 15 October 1927 (*in Elizabeth's name*) because the previous owner had just died. See *Metropolitan Nashville Register of Deeds*, 20737, bk. 716, 608.

10. Erik Barnouw, *A Tower in Babel: A History of Broadcasting in the United States, Volume 1–to 1933* (New York: Oxford University Press, 1966), 12–20 (hereinafter cited as Barnouw, *Tower in Babel*). In addition to contributing much of the early science on radio, Marconi was a shrewd businessman and would become very wealthy.

11. Ibid., 25–36, 43, 77.

12. Ibid., 69–71.

13. Ibid., 69–70, 80, 84, 105, 114, 125, 174, 209; Robert Sobel, *Coolidge: An American Enigma* (Washington, D.C.: Regnery Publishing, Inc., 1998), 248, 252, 310.

14. John H. DeWitt Jr., "Early Radio Broadcasting in Middle Tennessee," *Tennessee Historical Quarterly* 31 (spring 1972): 80–94 (hereinafter cited as DeWitt, "Early Radio Broadcasting"); "Nashville Historical Commission Marks First Radio Station Site at Belmont University," *Circle* 36 (fall/winter 1997–98): 10; Sykes DeWitt, telephone interview by author, 28 October 1998; Ward DeWitt Jr., telephone interview by author, 28 October 1998.

15. E. W.'s son, C. A. (Neil) II was in a Phi Delta Theta band at Vanderbilt. Francis Craig provided him saxophone lessons through his orchestra's reed man, Augie Clevenger.

16. "Industrial" insurance policies had small benefits and were usually sold to poor people, who had to pay weekly premiums. "Ordinary" insurance policies provided larger death benefits and were paid at quarterly or longer intervals.

17. George Hay, "History of WSM from the Memorable Inaugural Program October 5th, 1925," *Broadcast News of the Week*, 1, 12 November 1932, 3 (hereinafter cited as Hay, "History of WSM"); "Edwin Wilson Craig Rites at 3:30 Saturday," *NB*, 27 June 1969, 1, 2; "Craig, Giant of Insurance Industry, Dies," *NT*, 27 June 1969, 1, 14; "Funeral

Services Held for Edwin W. Craig, *Shield News*, 7 July 1969, 2.

18. Richard A. Peterson, "Industry Firm to Conglomerate Synergistics: Alternative Strategies for Selling Insurance and Country Music," in *Growing Metropolis* (Nashville: Vanderbilt University Press, 1975), 341–357.

19. "Radio Station Opens Tonight," *NB*, 5 October 1925, 1; "WSM Premiere Great Success," *NB*, 1, 6; "WSM Will Open Officially with Program Tonight," *NT*, 5 October 1925, 1, 8; Alvin Wiggers, "Nashville's Most Popular Musicians Help Make WSM Program Success," *NT*, 6 October 1925, 1, 16; Ingram MSS, 19, 20; Stamper, *National Life*, 115, 120–122; Hay, "History of WSM," 3, 5. No one has adequately preserved materials from or written the history of WSM, one of the nation's most important radio stations. Much of the materials referenced here were donated by Jesse Wills and reside in the WSM Radio & TV file, Rare Manuscripts Section, Vanderbilt Heard Library. These materials will be hereinafter cited as WSM file.

20. Brooks, "Nashville Profile," *NB*, 7 June 1945, 1; Marjorie Cooney, interview by author, 26 April 1998; Bill Kennon, telephone interview by author, 29 November 1998.

21. Francis narrated this story sometime in 1948 on a Hollywood radio show entitled "Meet the Music Makers."

22. Hay, "History of WSM," 9, 27; Ray Poindexter, *Golden Throats and Silver Tongues* (Conway, Ark.: River Road Press, 1978), 42, 50–51, 66; Charles K. Wolfe, *A Good-Natured Riot: The Birth of the Grand Ole Opry* (Nashville: The Country Music Foundation and Vanderbilt University Press, 1999), 7–11 (hereinafter cited as Wolfe, *A Good-Natured Riot*); Bobby Short remembered DeFord Bailey "sitting in" with Craig's band at the Grill Room. The uninterrupted broadcasting of *Opry* continues to this date.

23. DeWitt, "Early Radio Broadcasting"; William R. McDaniel, memo, March 1951, WSM file.

24. Rust, *Jazz Records 1897–1942*, 355–356.

25. Craig Papers; Sanjek and Sanjek, *American Popular Music*, 47; *Commodore*, 1930, features section; Francis Craig, interview by Ken Berryhill and Tom Landess, 24 January 1952, WMAK "Old Record Shop," Nashville; Lancaster, Sewanee, Tenn., letter to author, Nashville, 11 November 1998.

26. Broome and Tucker, *The Other Music City*.

27. Lancaster, interview, 28 March 1998.

28. Sanjek and Sanjek, *American Popular Music*, 66; Barnouw, *A Tower in Babel*, 233.

29. "Craig Will Play at Andrew Jackson," *NB*, undated article in Craig Papers; WSM radio schedule, *Nashville This Week*, 24–31 January 1927 and 2–9 April 1928; "The Andrew Jackson Hotel," *Nashville This Week*, 16–23 September 1929; WSM radio schedule, *Nashville This Week*, 3–10 March 1930. Much of the documentation about the band's performances comes from a chronological scrapbook of newspaper articles and advertisements which is cited as Craig Papers. Copies of these clippings in the Craig Papers were often undated.

30. "Snappy Tunes at Radio Show," *NB*, 27 August 1929, 1; Ibid., "Francis Craig Orchestra to Play at Banner Radio Show," *NB*, 28 August 1929, 1; "Nashville Radio," *NT*, 28 August 1929, 3; "Banner to Present Silver Loving Cup to Francis Craig at WSM Tonight," *NB*. (This undated clipping comes from the Craig Papers; it was probably in an early edition of the *Banner*, 21 April 1930); "Banner Cup Is Presented to Francis Craig at WSM," *NB*, 21 April 1930, 1.

31. Ingram MSS, 22; Elizabeth Romine, "In The Rockies"; "Plans For the Cap and Bells Show Announced, *Hustler*, 11 April 1930, 1, 2; "Cap and Bells Prospects Fine for Early Start," *Hustler*, 18 April 1930, 1; Lancaster, telephone interview, 24 November 1998. Another headline on page one of the 18 April 1930 *Hustler* was "Fugitives to Publish Book This Autumn." This alluded to *I'll Take My Stand: The South and the Agrarian Tradition*, the bible of the Agrarians. Lytle wrote an essay entitled "The Hind Tit" for the volume. He was also then working on his most famous book, *Bedford Forrest and His Critter Company*, which was published in 1931. The Lytle Papers are in the Special Collections Section of the Vanderbilt Heard Library.

32. "Amos 'n' Andy Continue to Lead with Nightly Broadcasts on WSM," *NB*, 18 May 1930, 9; Elizabeth Bryan, Nashville, letter to Francis Craig, Nashville, 8 May 1930, Craig Papers.

Chapter Three: Larghetto Poco a Poco

1. One of the publicity labels used for Craig during his heyday was "Dean of Southern Maestros."

2. Dr. Gewin died a wealthy man. His estate was divided into real estate and cash trusts. During the Depression, banks supposedly used the latter to satisfy mortgages on the former, leaving Mrs. Gewin a poor woman. She began working as a housemother at the Lambda Chi house at Auburn in the mid-1930s; Celeste Gewin Mitchiner, telephone interview by author, Mobile, Ala., 7 January 1999.

3. Roger M. DesPrez, "Tuberculosis Treatment—Old and New," Medicine Grand Rounds, Vanderbilt University School of Medicine, videocassette #M-1519, 25 May 1995; Mario C. Raviglione and Richard J. O'Brien, "Tuberculosis," in Harrison's Principles of Internal Medicine, ed. Anthony S. Favier et al. (New York: McGraw Hill, 1998), 1004–1014; Historical Statistics of the United States, Colonial Times to 1970, Washington, D.C.: U.S. Department of Commerce, 1975 (hereinafter cited as Historical Statistics); Mark Caldwell, The Last Crusade: The War on Consumption, 1862–1954 (New York: Atheneum, 1988), 9–11 (hereinafter cited as Caldwell, The Last Crusade); Stamper, National Life, 80–82; "Dr. W. C. Gewin, Prominent Here, Dies in Carolina," Birmingham Age-Herald, 16 July 1929, 1; James Radcliffe Squires, Allen Tate: A Literary Biography (New York: Pegasus, 1971), 36–41; Martin L. Dalton, "Blalock and Harrison—A Rare Friendship," Pharos of Alpha Omega Alpha, 61 (summer 1998): 26–31.

4. Caldwell, The Last Crusade, 3–15; "Confining for Cure," in Sheila M. Rothman, Living in the Shadow of Death (New York: BasicBooks, 1994), 194–210 (hereinafter cited as Rothman, Living in the Shadow).

5. Rothman, "The Sanatorium Narrative," in Living in the Shadow, 226–245; Caldwell, "Rules and a Daily Routine," in The Last Crusade, 67–97.

6. J. P. W. Brown, Nashville, letter to Francis Craig, Nashville, 13 May 1930; Mary Webb Haggard, Nashville, letter to Francis Craig, Denver, 23 May 1930; Robert James Craig, Nashville, letter to Francis Craig, Denver, 26 May 1930. These letters are in the Craig Papers. There are none from Francis.

7. Frances Melrose, "TB Victims Found Haven at Oakes," Denver Rocky Mountain News, Sunday, 3 April 1983, 14-N.

8. Lancaster, interview, 28 March 1998; Lancaster, telephone interviews, 24 November 1998, 7 January 1999; Mitchiner, telephone interview, Mobile,

Ala., 7 January 1999; Homer Gibbs Jr., telephone interview by author, Nashville, 25 January 1999.

9. Lancaster, interview, 28 March 1998; "First Dance Tonight," Hustler, 22 September 1930, 1.

10. Craig Papers.

11. Lancaster, telephone interview, 20 October 1998.

12. Among the friends who frequently came to Francis's aid were Dan Brooks, Bill Weaver, and Ed Webb.

13. Lancaster, interview, 28 January 1998; Lancaster, telephone interview, 6 July 1998; F. Clay Bailey Jr., telephone interview by author, 9 July 1998.

14. "Francis Craig Returns to WSM 'Mikes' with Rhythm Symphony," undated clipping in Craig Papers; "Tuning In," NB, 10 October 1931, 9 (The 6:30–6:45 P.M. slot on WSM's program was filled by "Francis Craig's Andrew Jackson Hotel Orchestra); University of Alabama Crimson-White, 15 March 1932; "Craig to Go on N.B.C. Hook-up," undated clipping in Craig Papers.

15. NBC's blue and red networks were based on lines drawn on a map in those colors depicting broadcast systems emanating from their stations WEAF (red) in New York City and WJZ (blue) in Newark, New Jersey. See Barnouw, A Tower in Babel, 191; Andrew W. Smith, "Following the Antenna," Birmingham News-Age-Herald; "Highlights on the Radio Today," Craig Papers.

16. Clint Garvin, telephone interviews by author, Moro Bay, Calif., 14 and 19 January 1999.

17. "Sounds Like a Press Agent's Yarn," Colorado City Post Telegram, Craig Papers.

18. Craig Papers; Garvin, telephone interview, 14 January 1999.

19. Craig Papers; Hay, "History of WSM," 12 November 1932, 7, 13.

20. Garvin, telephone interview, 2 April 1998.

21. Fifteenth Census, 873, 890.

22. Historical Statistics, 245; Corlew and Mitchell, Tennessee: A Short History, 514.

23. Doyle, Nashville in the New South, 223–232; Fred Colvin, "Caldwell and Company," in Tennessee Encyclopedia of History & Culture, ed. Carroll Van West (Nashville: Rutledge Hill Press, 1998), 110.

24. Robert G. Spinney, World War II in Nashville (Knoxville: University of Tennessee Press, 1998), 1, 2, 5 (hereinafter cited as Spinney, World War II in Nashville).

25. Sanjek and Sanjek, American Popular Music, 117–183.

26. "The Rise, the Glory and the Decline," in George Simon, *The Big Bands* (New York: Schirmer Books, 1981), 24–32 (hereinafter cited as Simon, *Big Bands*); Sawyer and Sawyer, "Big Bands," 24–28.
27. Garvin, interview, 26 January 1999.
28. Mary Jane Brooks, "Nashville Profile," *NB*, 7 June 1945, 1.
29. Craig Papers; "Craig's N.B.C. feature orchestra," *Hustler*, 10 February 1933, 1; Kennon, interview, 25 November 1998.
30. "Miss Elizabeth Craig Makes Bow at Brilliant Ball," *NB*, 28 December 1938, 1-X, 8-X; "Brilliant Debut Ball Is Given for Miss Fort," *NB*, 30 December 1938, 12.
31. Craig Papers; "M'Alister Will Be Inaugurated With Ceremonies Today," *NT*, 16 January 1936, 1, 5; "Reception and Inaugural Ball Are Given at Hermitage Hotel," *NB*, 17 January 1935, 4.
32. "Melton Welcomed By Many Friends; Praises Teacher," *NB*, 26 November 1935, 1; "Phone Keeps Melton Busy," *NB*, 8; "Governor Welcomes Melton," *NB*, 27 November 1935, 11; "James Melton Honored at Banquet," *NB*, 28 November 1935, 9.
33. Garvin, telephone interview, 19 January 1999.
34. *Historical Statistics*, pt. 2, 796; Craig Papers; Stamper, *National Life*, 127; "Edwin Wilson Craig Rites at 3:30 Saturday," *NB*, 27 June 1969, 1, 2.
35. "Francis Craig Piping Majors Up from Dixie," *New York Enquirer*, 23 May 1937, Craig Papers.
36. Corinne Dale, telephone interview by author, Nashville, 27 April 1999.
37. Bill Barry, interview by author, 26 February 1998; Celeste Craig Abernathy, interview by author, 6 May 1998; Walt Summers, telephone interview by author, Nashville, 19 November 1998; Kennon, telephone interview, 29 November 1998; Garvin, telephone interview, 26 January 1999.
38. Beverly LeCroy, telephone interview by author, 26 January 1999.
39. The sexual identifications of band vocalists might seem demeaning to some late twentieth-century readers. However, in the dance band era, they were called "boy" or "girl" singers. Amazingly, they apparently did not even seem to resent the aspersions on their maturity.
40. Ben Austin, *The 40 Year Cycle* (South Pasadena, Calif.: The Kilmarnock Press, 1980), (hereinafter cited as Austin, *The 40 Year Cycle*).
41. Russell and Maxwell, *Fifty Years of Vanderbilt Football*.

42. Barry, interview, 26 February 1998; Garvin, interview, 2 April 1998; Jud Collins, interview by author, Nashville, 28 April 1998.
43. "New Marching Song, Key Vanderbilt Figures in Thanksgiving Classic," *Hustler*, 23 November 1938, 1; "When Vandy Starts to Fight," *Hustler*, 2; E. M. Haywood, telephone interview by author, Nashville, 24 August 1998; Dwayne Sagen, telephone interview by author, 26 January 1999. There was an attempt to introduce another fight song in 1941, something called "Vanderbilt Salute," by Mack Allaman. Perhaps this was the basis for the incorrect composition date for "Dynamite" on the historical marker in front of Francis's home. See "Band to Introduce Vandy Fight Song," *Hustler*, 38 November 1941, 1.
An undergraduate fraternity brother of Francis Craig, Joe C. Landess, donated another successful fight song to Vanderbilt in 1953, the year of his son Tom's graduation. "Cheer For Old Vandy" was originally written for Tom's undergraduate school, Deerfield. Tom disliked that place so much, though, that his father gave it to Vanderbilt. It is often used but has never replaced "Dynamite." Tom Landess, telephone interviews by author, 22 October 1998 and 26 January 1999.
Because of confusion engendered by the text of "Dynamite" and students' inability to remember the words, there was a movement on the campus in the mid-1990s to have a contest to change them. Nothing came of that. Sagen, interview, 26 January 1999.
44. Marjorie Kirby, interview by author, 12 June 1999.
45. Elizabeth Proctor, interview by author, 29 April 1998; Alice Holcomb, interview by author, 26 August 1998; Doris Kelly, telephone interview by author, 26 January 1999. In a downhome fashion, Francis's radio broadcasts were also sometimes personalized. When Lillian Dobson's brother John was born on 1 January 1937, Francis played "Oh, Johnny" on the air. Lillian Dunnavant, telephone interview by author, Memphis, 3 February 1998.
46. Lancaster, interview, 28 March 1998; Garvin, interviews, 5 February 1998 and 2 April 1998; Dick Dudley, telephone interview by author, Willow Street, Pa., 10 January 1999; Kelly, telephone interview, Nashville, 26 January 1999.
47. Donia Dickerson, interview by author, 31 January 1998; Lancaster, interviews,

28 March 1998, 6 July 1999; Bailey, telephone interview, 9 July 1998; John Hardcastle, telephone interview by author, Nashville, 30 January 1999; copy of Craig installment deed; "Nostalgia News Report," *Pages of Time 1938*, Millersville, Tenn., n.p.

48. Mary Jane Brooks, "Nashville Profile," *NB*, 7 June 1945, 1; Lancaster, telephone interview, 4 February 1999.

49. The musicians sometimes frequented more hip clubs after work in order to "sit in" on music more interesting to them.

50. Francis's wealthy cousins and uncles were never anything other than proud and supportive of him.

51. Don Doyle, *Nashville since the 1920s* (Knoxville: University of Tennessee Press, 1985), 110–115; *Historical Statistics of the United States*, part 1, 245; Spinney, *World War II in Nashville*, 20–22.

52. Doyle, *Nashville since the 1920s*, 110–115; Spinney, *World War II in Nashville*, 77–83.

53. Craig registration card, Craig Papers.

54. Francis Craig, letter to Howard Baughman, Nashville, 28 April 1944, Craig Papers.

55. WSM papers; Doyle, *Nashville since the 1920s*, 146.

56. Dolly Dearman, interview by author, Nashville, 2 June 1998; Dearman, telephone interview, 11 January 1999; LeCroy, telephone interview, 10 July 1998; Anne Parman, interview by author, 26 September 1998; Brooks, "Nashville Profile," 7 June 1945, 1.

57. "D. J. Plus A. & R. Equal V. I. P.," in Meyer, *The Gold in Tin Pan Alley*, 124–153; Sanjek and Sanjek, *American Popular Music*, 51, 61; Barnouw, *A History of Broadcasting*, 218–219.

58. "They're Playing Our Song," in Meyer, *The Gold in Tin Pan Alley*, 76–106; Doyle, *Nashville since the 1920s*, 154; "Funeral Services Held for Edwin W. Craig, *Shield News*, 7 July 1969, 2; Bill Baird and Bill Barry interview by the author, Nashville, 26 February 1998; Kinkle, *Popular Music and Jazz*, xxxviii, xxxix.

59. Tapes of various Craig broadcasts; "Craig Band Broadcasts from Here," *Cherry Point Wind Sock*, 15 June 1946, 1.

60. Garvin, interview, 5 February 1998; Alfred Bartles, telephone interview by author, Nashville, 13 April 1999.

61. Eric Partridge, *A Dictionary of Slang and Unconventional English*, ed. Paul Beale (London: Routledge and Kegan Paul, 8th ed., 1984), 252, 548, 1187.

62. Kinkle, *Popular Music and Jazz*, xxxix; Simon, *The Big Bands*, 31, 32; Hamm, *Yesterdays: Popular Song*, 386–387; Mary Jane Brooks, "Nashville Profile," *NB*, 7 June 1945, 1; "Pat Anderson, "Now and Then with Nashville Music Men," *NT*, 2 July 1961; Parman, telephone interview, Nashville, 26 September 1998.

63. Cooney, interview, 26 April 1998; Cooney, telephone interview, 8 February 1999; Christine Smith, telephone interviews by author, 27 April 1998, 15 January 1999; Dick Dudley, interview by author, 10 January 1999; Kirby, telephone interview, 13 July 1999.

64. "D. J. Plus A. & R. Equal V. I. P.," in Meyer, *The Gold in Tin Pan Alley*, 124–153; Barnouw, *A History of Broadcasting*, 216–219; Collins, interview, 28 April 1998.

65. Craig Papers.

Chapter Four: Allegro ma non troppo

1. John Rumble, "The Emergence of Nashville as a Recording Center, Logbooks from the Castle Studio, 1952–1953," *Journal of Country Music* (December 1978): 22–41 (hereinafter cited as Rumble, "The Emergence of Nashville as a Recording Center"); Wolfe, *A Good-Natured Riot*, 169–175; Aaron Shelton, interview by author, New Johnsonville, Tenn., 7 May 1998. Shelton later taught math classes at Vanderbilt for several years.

2. Script of WSM interview of Francis Craig, Craig Papers; "D. J. Plus A. & R. Equal V. I. P., in Meyer, *The Gold in Tin Pan Alley*, 124–153; Lillian Dunnavant, telephone interview by author, Memphis, Tenn., 3 February 1998; Rachel (Mrs. Jim) Bulleit, telephone interview by author, Safety Harbor, Fla., 6 February 1998; Jay Orr and Tom Roland, "Music Gave Nashville Identity," *NT*, 3 January 1999, 1A, 10–11A, hereinafter cited as Orr and Roland, "Nashville Identity"; Aaron Shelton, "The Story of Castle Recording Lab," in *Autobiography* (n.p., 1990 [?]), 161–167 (hereinafter cited as Shelton, "Castle Recording"). The noted chapter is in the Nashville Room of the Nashville Metropolitan Library, main branch. Shelton's book is unpublished.

3. Laura Eipper, "'Near You' Still on Top after All These Years," *NT*, 20 March 1977, 1F, 2F; Red O'Donnell, "Goell's 'Near You' Is Still a Big Seller," *NB*, 14 October 1971, 18; Patricia (Goell) Newcastle, telephone interview

by author, New York, N.Y., 3 April 1998. Mrs. Newcastle was twice married to Kermit Goell.

4. Shelton, "Castle Recording"; John Rumble, "Fred Rose and the Development of the Nashville Music Industry" (Ph.D. diss., Vanderbilt University, 1980).

5. At a longer session on 13 February 1947, Castle recorded four sides for Sterling and Hank Williams, including the first issue of one of his hits, "Honky Tonkin'."

6. Shelton, "Castle Recording"; Shelton, interview, 7 May 1998; "WSM's Francis Craig in National Music Spotlight," *Our Shield*, 22 September 1947, 3; Francis Craig WSM interview text, Craig Papers; untitled newspaper clipping, *NB*, February 1970.

7. Bulleit, interview, 6 February 1998; Bill Holder, "Bullet Hits the Bull's Eye," *Nashville Tennessean Magazine*, 28 March 1948, 6, 7 (hereinafter cited as Holder, "Bullet Hits the Bull's Eye").

8. "Record Possibilities," *Billboard*, 7 August 1947, 33; 30 August 1947; "Small Diskers in Heyday with Million Sales," New York, 6 September 1947, undated clipping, Craig Papers.

9. Shelton, "Castle Recording."

10. "Francis Craig's New Tune 'Near You' Sensational Nation-Wide Hit," *Ragland Reporter*, October 1947, 9–13; Joel Whitburn, *Joel Whitburn's Pop Memories 1890–1954: The History of American Popular Music* (Menomonee Falls, Wis.: Record Research Inc., 1986), 627 (hereinafter cited as *Whitburn's Pop Memories*); *Variety*, various tabulations, 17 September 1947–10 January 1948.

11. John R. Williams, *This Was "Your Hit Parade"* (Rockland, Minn.: Courier-Gazette, Inc., 1973), 3–5, 8, 14 (hereinafter cited as Williams, *"Your Hit Parade"*); Francis Hill Tanberg, Seattle, letter to program director, *Lucky Strike Hit Parade*, New York, 1 November 1947, Craig Papers.

12. *Whitburn's Pop Memories*, 102; *Ragland Reporter*, October 1947, 12.

13. "The Story Behind the Song," in "Juke Box Comics," (New York: Famous Funnies, Inc..), September 1948; Kennon, interview, 20 November 1998.

14. "Craig's WM Tour Marks Latest Disk to Ducat Success," newspaper clipping, Craig Papers, 20 September 1947; Paul Jones, "Backstage," newspaper article, Craig Papers; Paul Lenk, interview by author, Nashville, 29 May 1998.

15. Articles and bills, Craig Papers; Francis Craig, interview by Jo Sherman, WSM, 1962; Lancaster and Dickerson, interviews by the author, 18 January 1998.

16. *Billboard*, 27 December 1947, 29; *Billboard*, 24 January 1948, 48; "Looks Like 'Pardon' Will Duplicate 'Near You' Sale," *Variety* article, Craig Papers. Beasley Smith's decision to pursue a career as a composer allowed him to leave the grind of leading a band on the road. He published ninety-eight songs, many of them hits.

17. *Whitburn's Pop Memories*, 102; Williams, *"Your Hit Parade,"* 153, 154; *Billboard*, 3 January 1948, 18–20; *Time*, 12 January 1948, 34; "Francis Craig Impresses Folk Here As Southern Gentleman," newspaper article, Craig Papers; other clippings, Craig Papers.

18. Dickerson, interview, 18 January 1998; Lancaster, telephone interview, 24 May 1999; "City Council Honors Craig," undated clipping in Craig Papers; WSM radio interview, n.d.; Ingram MSS. The only four people previously so honored by the council had been Tony Sudekum, C. A. Craig, A. M. Burton, and Joe Werthan.

19. "Song Writer Becomes Booster," newspaper article, Craig Papers; "WJHP PARAGRAPHS," Craig Papers; Bob Healey, Bullet Recording Co. catalog, folder in Country Music Hall of Fame library.

20. Newcastle, telephone interviews, New York, 3 April 1998, 17 November 1998.

21. He presumably left Bullet because he got a better deal.

22. Shelton, "Castle Recording"; Shelton, telephone interview, 23 February 1999; Shelton, interview, 7 May 1998; "A New Big Sound Blows Out of Nashville," *Broadcasting*, 28 January 1963, 67–69; Robyn Flans, "The History of Nashville Recording," *Mix*, March 1988, 66–77; Rumble, "The Emergence of Nashville as a Recording Center," 22–41. In 1983, Castle Recording's version of Hank Williams's "Your Cheatin' Heart" on the MGM label was put into the Hall of Fame of the National Academy of Recording Arts and Sciences.

23. Lomax, *Nashville Music City USA*, 8.

24. Kinkle, *Popular Music and Jazz*, xi, 437–438.

25. *Whitburn's Pop Memories*, 627; Joel Whitburn, *Billboard 1995 Music Yearbook* (Menomenee Falls, Wis.: Record Research, Inc., 1996), 31; Alex, *Billboard* records department, telephone conversation with

author, New York, 27 April 1999.
26. Layng Martine Jr., letter to author, Nashville, 10 June 1998.
27. Dale Cockrell, telephone interview by author, Nashville, 26 March 1999. Cockrell is a musicologist at Vanderbilt's Blair School of Music.
28. Beegie Adair, interview by author, Nashville, 24 March 1999.
29. Bob McDill, letter to author, Nashville, 6 February 1999.
30. Bart Durham, interview by author, Nashville, 23 April 1998; *Cigar Classics, Volume One, The Standards* (Universal City, Calif.: Universal Music Special Markets, Inc., 1997), compact disc.
31. Sony Music did not give permission to use this beautiful rendition on the Francis Craig CD in this volume.
32. O'Donnell, "Goell's 'Near You' Is Still A Big Seller," *NB*, 14 October 1971, 18; *Joel Whitburn's Top Country Singles 1944–1993* (Menomenee Falls, Wis.: Record Research, Inc., 1994), 432, 509, 593; Tom Roland, "Queen of Heartache Dies," *NT*, 7 April 1998, 1A, 5A; Hamm, *Yesterdays: Popular Song*, 338, 487–488; Beverly Keel, "Mr. Guitar," *Nashville Life* (December, January 1998), 62–67 (hereinafter cited as Keel, "Mr. Guitar"); Roland and Orr, "'The A Team,'" *NT*, 21 June 1998, 1K-3K. Country performers singing "crossover" popular ballads were in vogue at this time. Willy Nelson's *Stardust* album was released in 1978.
33. McDill, correspondence, 6 February 1999; Billy Rose, "'Joe' Named 'Ike,'" clipping, Craig Papers.
34. Pat Anderson, "Now and Then with Nashville Music Men," *NT*, 2 July 1961.
35. Craig Papers; Sydney Dalton, "Composer Craig's New March Banner Jubilee Music Praised," *NB*, n.d. The brave words of the *Banner* march (on CD) are especially ironic since the newspaper failed in February 1998. The record did not sell all that well. Staffers would light firecrackers in the disk spindle holes of discs and hurl them into the *Tennessean* newsroom. See Henry Walker, "Death Blow," *Nashville Scene*, 19 February 1998, 27.
36. "Francis Craig to Be Honored in Washington," *NB*, n.d.
37. "Song Suit 'Ridiculous' Francis Craig Says," *NT*, 13 November 1952, 16; "U.S. Court Dismisses Suit over Hit Tune," *NT*, 2 April 1953, 27; *Jones v. Supreme Music Corp. et al.*, United States District Court S. D. New York, November 8, 1951; *Jones v. Craig* No. 11948, United States Court of Appeals Sixth Circuit, April 30, 1954; Bailey, telephone interview, 9 July 1998.

38. Irving Waugh, interview by author, 10 June 1998; Doug Henry, interview by author, 17 July 1998; Haywood, telephone interview, Nashville, 24 August 1998; Ken Berryhill, telephone interview by author, Nashville, 29 October 1998; Rosie Smith Minton, telephone interview by author, Gallatin, Tenn., 27 January 1999.
39. "Home Office Shield," July 1954, 3, 4. Checkpoint Charley in Berlin was supposedly named for Francis's brother, Charles.
40. Lancaster, Sewanee, letter to author, Nashville, 17 March 1999.
41. Dorothy Kilgallen, "Broadway," *Pittsburgh Post-Gazette*, 3 December 1947, Craig Papers; Bart Durham, interview, Nashville, 23 April 1998; Jonathan Goell, facsimile to author, 2 May 1999.
42. Rachel Bulleit, interview, 6 February 1998; Bulleit, 15 March 1999; Holder, "Bullet Hits the Bull's Eye"; Keel, "Mr. Guitar," 66; Orr and Roland, "Nashville Identity," 11A; "Bullet Recording and Transcription Co.," compilation by Joe Nicholas, Country Music Hall of Fame archives, c. 1957; Ken Clee, *The Directory of American 45 R.P.M. Records* (Nashville: Country Music Hall of Fame, 1985); Ozell Simpkins, telephone interview by author, Nashville, 5 April 1999; Bill Friskies-Warren, "Voices Raised, the Uplifting Enduring Harmonies of the Fairfield Four," *Nashville Scene*, 26 February 1998, 20–27.
43. "Statistical Record of Nashville 1966–1967," Nashville Area Chamber of Commerce. For a depiction of the student civil rights movement in Nashville in the 1960s, see David Halberstam, *The Children* (New York: Random House, 1998).
44. "Composer Francis Craig's Funeral Services Held," *NB*, 21 November 1966, 1, 3; "Francis Craig," *NB* 18; "Famed Composer, Orchestra Leader Francis Craig Dies," *NT*, 21 November 1966, 1, 2; "Francis Craig," *New York Times*, 21 November 1966, 45; Kermit Goell, letter to Elizabeth Craig, Nashville, 23 November 1966.
45. Bartles, interview, 13 April 1999; David Humphreys, telephone interview by author, Nashville 29 April 1999. For a thoroughly overwrought article on the 1999 swing movement, see Juliette Guilbert, "Backward Thinking," *Nashville Scene*, 10 June 1999, 32–37.
46. LeCroy, interview, 23 March 1998; Brad Schmidt, "Brad About You," *NT*, 28 January 1999, 3A.
47. Rich Riebling, "Hermitage Hotel Renovation Planned," *NB*, 2 September

1977, 18; Albert Cason, "Hotel Work Papers Inked," *NT*, 25 June 1980, 26; Hieronymus, "The Hermitage: An Aging Beauty Recovers Status," *NT*, 4 February 1981, 35, 38.

48. Will Beasley, *Nashville Music City USA*, Nashville's Partnership 2000 (Nashville: Nashville Chamber of Commerce, n.d.); Keel, "Broken Records," *Nashville Scene*, 11 February 1999, 20–21; Keel, "Fit And Working Again," *Scene*, 22–23.

49. Robert S. Lancaster, *The Better Parts of a Life*, (Sewanee, Tenn.: Proctor's Hall Press, 1990), 206; Lancaster, interview, Nashville, 20 April 1999.

Chapter Five: Ripresa
1. Don Doyle, *New Men, New Cities, New South* (Chapel Hill: University of North Carolina Press, 1990), 208–213.

2. These opinions come from numerous of Francis's former musicians.

3. Simon, *Big Bands*, 312–317.

4. Jonathan Goell, telephone interview, Takoma Park, Md., 2 April 1998.

5. "Payola!" in Meyer, *The Gold in Tin Pan Alley*, 154–185; "Payola and the Celler Hearings," in Sanjek and Sanjek, *American Popular Music*, 155–195.

6. Lancaster, interview, 28 March 1998; Bartles, interview, 13 April 1999.

7. The author thanks the Reverend Michael E. Williams for instruction on Methodist theology. Williams, telephone interview by author, Nashville, 29 June 1999.

Chapter Six: Francis Craig Orchestra Graduates
1. Craig Papers; Irene Beasley Papers, University of Maryland Libraries.

2. Ingram MSS, 15; *Birmingham News-Age-Herald*, 7 February 1937, 11, 15; Simon, *Big Bands*, 497; Robert McG. Thomas Jr., "Phil Harris, 91, Band Leader and Radio Comedian, Dies," *New York Times Biographical Service*, 14 August 1995, 1174; Fred Russell, "Remembering When Phil Harris Was a Mirthful Nashville Teenager," *NB*, 17 August 1995, E-3; Bivin, "I Remember."

3. Kinkle, *Popular Music and Jazz*, 1240; Margo Melton Nutt (James Melton's daughter), telephone interview by author, Fairlee, Vt., 29 November 1998; *Central Florida Ocala Times*, newspaper clipping, courtesy of Margo Nutt; "James Melton, A '25," *Vanderbilt Alumnus*, December 1942, 3; "James Melton," *Vanderbilt Alumnus*, September–October 1961, 31; "James Melton, 57, Noted Tenor, Dies," *New York Times*, 23 April 1961, 86; "James Melton," *NB*, 24 April 1961, 8; John Bridges, "Signor de Luca Taught Nashville How to Sing," *NT*, 29 September 1985, 1F, 9F; Lancaster interviews, 18 January 1998 and 28 March 1998; Nutt, Fairlee, Vt., letter to author, 5 April 1999; John Dunning, *Tune in Yesterday* (Englewood Cliffs, N.J.: Prentice-Hall, Inc., 1976), 524–525. Despite claims from the various universities he attended, Melton never won a degree, either from Vanderbilt or the Universities of Florida and Georgia.

4. Kinkle, *Popular Music and Jazz*, 1706–1707; Broome and Tucker, *The Other Music City*; Simon, *Big Bands*, 117–123; Simon, *Simon Says*, 45–47; Bivin, "I Remember."

5. Snooky Lanson's name was later changed. I use his given name until that time in the narrative.

6. Kinkle, *Popular Music and Jazz*, 1291–1292; WAMB radio broadcast testimonial to Snooky Lanson, done the week after his death 3 July 1990; Garvin, interview, 23 February 1998; Barry, interview, 26 February 1998; Beth Landman Roach, interview by author, Franklin, Tenn., 29 May 1998; Roach, interviews, 7 July 1998 and 24 March 1999; Dudley, interview, 10 January 1999. Careful research of ownership records of the Hermitage Hotel revealed no connection to National Life executives or their company.

7. Craig, Craig Papers; Earl Wilson, "Peewee's Been on Broadway 35 Years," *Asheville Citizen Times*, 1 April 1975; Bivin, "I Remember"; Lancaster, interview, 31 January 1998; Barry, interview, 26 February 1998; Will T. Malone, Donelson, interview by author, 16 March 1998; Bailey, interview, 9 July 1998; Kennon, interview, 29 November 1998; Dudley, interview, 10 January 1999; Garvin, interview, 14 January 1999.

8. Simon, *Simon Says*, 350–353; Kinkle, *Popular Music and Jazz*, 1747–1748; Austin, *The 40 Year Cycle*, 63, 67, 92; Charlie Appleton, "Dinah Still Held Dear in Tennessee Hearts," *NB*, A-1, A-2, 25 February 1994; Appleton, "We'll Miss Dinah," *NB*, A-12; Ken Beck, "Goodbye to the Girl Next Door," *NT*, 1, 25 February 1994; Sandy Smith and Linda Quigley, "Dinah Shore: All-American Girl," *NT*, 7A; Garvin, interviews, 5 February 1998 and 23 February 1998; Cooney, interview, 26 April 1998; Shelton, interview, 7 May 1998; Miriam Cowden, telephone interview by author, Nashville,

24 August 1998; Greer Ricketson, telephone interview by author, 5 January
1999; Dinah Shore, Los Angeles, letter to
Mr. and Mrs. Ed Kirby, Nashville, 21
June 1971.

9. Kinkle, *Popular Music and Jazz*, 1216;
Simon, *Big Bands*, 156, 274, 424,
430–432; Gino Falzarano, "The Kitty
Kallen Story," Sony Music Entertainment,
1992; "Time for T," Joe Showler,
Producer/Writer, Vernon Films, MCS
Recording Studio, Toronto; Garvin, inter-
views, 5 February 1998, 23 February
1998, 5 May 1998, 14 January 1999;
Barry, interview, 26 February 1998; Kitty
Kallen, telephone interview by author,
Englewood, N. J., 23 April 1998; Collins,
interview, 28 April 1998; Shelton, inter-
view, 7 May 98; E. D. Thompson, "WSM
Radio, Much More Than the Opry!"
Westview, 24 June 1999,2.

10. Broome and Tucker, *The Other Music
City*; Lenk, interview, 29 May 1998; Mrs.
Bob Johnstone, telephone interview by
author, Nashville, 17 November 1998; E. D.
Thompson, "WSM Radio Much More
Than the Opry!" *Westview*, 24 June 1999, 2.

Discography
1. Brian Rust, *The American Dance Band
Discography, 1917–1942*, vol. 1 (New Rochelle,
N. Y.: Arlington House, 1978), 755–756;
Rust, *Jazz Records*, 355–356; Kinkle, *Popular
Music and Jazz*, 756; *MCA Records, Inc.
Historical Catalogue*, vol. 2, Universal City,
Calif., 31 December 1979, 525; Broome and
Tucker, *The Other Music City*.

2. The first tune was also released on
Regal G-8744 as the Raymond Dance
Band, the second on Columbia 4134 as
the Denza Dance Band.

Catalogue
1. This song was attributed to Francis
Craig and Kermit Goell on a 1955 Dot
recording of both. It was never published.

2. This unpublished song was on the
flip side of Craig's only known Dot record.

Bibliography

Books

Austin, Ben. *The 40 Year Cycle.* South Pasadena, California: The Kilmarnock Press, 1980.

Barnouw, Erik. *The Golden Web: A History of Broadcasting in the United States. Volume 2, 1933 to 1953.* New York: Oxford University Press, 1968.

———. *A Tower in Babel: A History of Broadcasting in the United States, Volume 1–to 1933.* New York: Oxford University Press, 1966.

Broome, Paul J., and Clay Tucker. *The Other Music City: The Bands and Jazz Musicians of Nashville,1920 to 1970.* Nashville: American Press Print, 1990.

Caldwell, Mark. *The Last Crusade: The War on Consumption, 1862–1954.* New York: Atheneum, 1988.

Chase, Gilbert. *America's Music from Pilgrims to the Present.* 3d ed. Urbana, Ill.: University of Illinois Press, 1987.

Clee, Ken. *The Directory of American 45 R.P.M. Records.* Nashville: Country Music Foundation and Media Center, 1985.

Colvin, Fred. *Tennessee Encyclopedia of History & Culture.* Edited by Carroll Van West. Nashville: Rutledge Hill Press, 1998.

Conkin, Paul K. *Gone with the Ivy: A Biography of Vanderbilt University.* Knoxville: The University of Tennessee Press, 1985.

Corlew, Robert Ewing. *A History of Dickson County Tennessee.* The Tennessee Historical Commission and The Dickson County Historical Society, 1956.

Davis, Ronald L. *The Modern Era, 1920–Present.* Vol. 3 of *A History of Music in American Life.* Malabar, Fla.: Robert Krieger Publishing Company, 1981.

Donaldson, Mary Louise. *A History of the Vanderbilt School of Nursing.* Nashville: Vanderbilt University Press, 1985.

Doyle, Don H. *Nashville in the New South, 1880–1930.* Knoxville: University of Tennessee Press, 1985.

———. *Nashville since the 1920s.* Knoxville: University of Tennessee Press, 1985.

———. *New Men, New Cities, New South.* Chapel Hill: University of North Carolina Press, 1990.

Dunning, John. *Tune in Yesterday.* Englewood Cliffs, N.J.: Prentice-Hall, Inc., 1976.

Durham, Walter. *A History of the First United Methodist Church, Gallatin, Tennessee.* Gallatin, Tenn.: n.p., 1984.

Folmsbee, Stanley J., Robert E. Corlew, and Enoch L. Mitchell. *Tennessee: A Short History.* Knoxville: The University of Tennessee Press, 1972.

Garrett, Jill Knight. *Dickson County Handbook.* N.p.: Southern Historical Press, Inc., 1984.

Hamm, Charles. *Yesterdays: Popular Song in America.* New York: W. W. Norton & Company, 1979.

Kinkle, Roger. *The Complete Encyclopedia of Popular Music and Jazz, 1900–1950.* 4 vols. New Rochelle, N.Y.: Arlington House, 1974.

Lancaster, Robert S. *The Better Parts of a Life.* Sewanee, Tenn.: Proctor's Hall Press, 1990.

Lomax, John III. *Nashville Music City USA.* New York: Harry N. Abrams, Inc., 1985.

McGaw, Robert A. *A Brief History of Vanderbilt University.* Nashville: Vanderbilt University, 1973.

Meyer, Hazel. *The Gold in Tin Pan Alley.* Philadelphia: J. B. Lippincott Company, 1958.

Mims, Edwin. *Chancellor Kirkland of Vanderbilt.* Nashville: Vanderbilt University Press, 1940.

———. *History of Vanderbilt University.* Nashville: Vanderbilt University Press, 1946.

Moore, John Trotwood, and Austin P. Foster. *Tennessee, The Volunteer State, 1760–1923.* Vol. 1. Nashville: S. J. Clarke Publishing Company, 1923.

Partridge, Eric. *A Dictionary of Slang and Unconventional English.* 8th ed. London: Routledge and Kegan Paul, 1984.

Peterson, Richard A. *Growing Metropolis.* Nashville: Vanderbilt University Press, 1975.

Pittard, Mabel. *Rutherford County.* Tennessee County History Series. Memphis: Memphis State University Press, 1985.

Poindexter, Ray. *Golden Throats and Silver Tongues.* Conway, Ark.: River Road Press, 1978.

Raviglione, Mario C., and Richard J. O'Brien. *Harrison's Principles of Internal Medicine.* Edited by Anthony S. Favier et al. New York: McGraw Hill, 1998.

Reynolds, Morgan B. *Seventy Years of Belle Meade Country Club, 1901–1971.* Nashville: McQuiddy Printing Co., 1971.

Rothman, Sandra. *Living in the Shadow of Death*. New York: BasicBooks, 1994.

Russell, Fred, and Benson Maxwell. *Fifty Years of Vanderbilt Football*. Nashville: n.p., 1938.

Rust, Brian. *The American Dance Band Discography, 1917–1942*. Vol. 1. New Rochelle, N. Y.: Arlington House, 1975.

———. *Jazz Records, 1897–1942*. Vol. 1. New Rochelle, N. Y.: Arlington House, 1978.

Sablosky, Irving. *American Music*. Chicago: University of Chicago Press, 1969.

Sanjek, Russell, and David Sanjek. *American Popular Music Business in the 20th Century*. New York: Oxford University Press, 1991.

Simon, George T. *The Big Bands*. New York: Schirmer Books, 1981.

———. *Glenn Miller and His Orchestra*. New York: Thomas Y. Crowell Company, 1974.

Simpson, J. A., and E. S. C. Weiner. *The Oxford English Dictionary*, 2d ed. Vol. 8. Oxford: Clarendon Press, 1989.

Sobel, Robert. *Coolidge: An American Enigma*. Washington, D.C.: Regnery Publishing, Inc., 1998.

Spinney, Robert G. *World War II in Nashville*. Knoxville: University of Tennessee Press, 1998.

Squires, James Radcliffe. *Allen Tate: A Literary Biography*. New York: Pegasus, 1971.

Stamper, Powell. *The National Life Story*. New York: Appleton-Century-Crofts, 1968.

Tidwell, Oscar Cromwell, Jr. *Belle Meade Park*. Nashville: n.p., 1983.

Whitburn, Joel. *Joel Whitburn's Pop Memories 1890–1954: The History of American Popular Music*. Menomonee Falls, Wis.: Record Research Inc., 1986.

———. *Joel Whitburn's Top Country Singles 1944–1993*. Menomonee Falls, Wis.: Record Research, Inc., 1994.

Williams, John R. *This Was "Your Hit Parade."* Rockland, Minn.: Courier-Gazette, Inc., 1973.

Wilson, R. Jackson, and others. *The Pursuit of Liberty: A History of the American People*. 2d d. Belmont, Calif.: Wadsworth Publishing Company: 1990.

Wolfe, Charles K. *A Good-Natured Riot: The Birth of the Grand Ole Opry*. Nashville: The Country Music Foundation and Vanderbilt University Press, 1999.

Interviews and Letters

Abernathy, Celeste Craig (Murfreesboro, Tennessee)
Abernathy, Lane (Murfreesboro)
Adair, Beegie (Nashville)
Bailey, F. Clay, Jr., (Nashville)
Baird, Bill (Nashville)
Barry, Bill (Nashville)
Bartles, Alfred (Nashville)
Berryhill, Ken (Nashville)
Black, Mary Elizabeth (Tallahassee, Florida)
Bowen, Cawthon, Jr. (Nashville)
Bradley, Harold (Nashville)
Bulleit, Rachel (Safety Harbor, Florida)
Byrd, B. F., Jr. (Nashville)
Caldwell, Wentworth, Jr. (Nashville)
Clark, Sherri (Colorado Springs, Colorado)
Cockrell, Dale (Nashville)
Collins, Jud (Nashville)
Cooney, Marjorie (Nashville)
Cowden, Miriam (Nashville)
Crabtree, Bruce (Nashville)
Craig, C. A., II (Nashville)
Cunningham, Ruth (Nashville)
Dale, Corinne (Nashville)
Denny, Dolly Dearman (Nashville)
DeWitt, Jack (Nashville)
DeWitt, Sykes (Nashville)
DeWitt, Ward, Jr. (Nashville)
Dickerson, Donia Craig (Nashville)
Dudley, Dick (Willow Street, Pennsylvania)
Dunnavant, Lillian (Memphis)
Durham, Bart (Nashville)
Garvin, Clint (Moro Bay, California)
Gewin, Henry (Mobile, Alabama)
Gibbs, Homer, Jr. (Nashville)
Goell, Jonathan (Takoma Park, Maryland)
Hardcastle, John (Nashville)
Haywood, E. M. (Nashville)
Henry, Douglas (Nashville)
Holcomb, Alice (Nashville)
Howell, Charlie (Nashville)
Humphreys, David (Nashville)
Johnstone, Georgia (Nashville)
Kallen, Kitty (Englewood, New Jersey)
Keeble, Alice (Monteagle, Tennessee)
Kelly, Doris (Nashville)
Kennon, Bill (Nashville)
Kieman, Wanda (New York)
Kirby, Marjorie Arnold (Nashville)
Lancaster, Elizabeth Gewin Craig (Nashville and Sewanee, Tennessee)
Landess, Tom (Columbia, South Carolina)
Law, Pamela (Sewanee, Tennessee)
LeCroy, Beverly (Nashville)

Lenk, Paul (Nashville)
Lomax, John, III (Nashville)
Malone, Will T. (Donelson, Tennessee)
Martine, Layng, Jr. (Nashville)
McDill, Bob (Nashville)
McElhiney, Bill (Diamond Head, Mississippi)
Military, Frank (New York)
Minton, Rosie Smith (Gallatin, Tennessee)
Mitchiner, Celeste Gewin (Mobile, Alabama)
Newcastle, Patricia (Goell) (New York)
Nutt, Margo Melton (Fairlee, Vermont)
Parman, Anne Vaughn (Nashville)
Patrick, Pat (Nashville)
Proctor, Elizabeth (Nashville)
Pugh, Ronnie (Nashville)
Ragland, Mary Cortner (Nashville)
Ricketson, Greer (Nashville)
Roach, Beth Landman (Franklin, Tennessee)
Robinson, Margaret Ann (Nashville)
Rumble, John (Nashville)
Russell, Fred (Nashville)
Sagen, Dwayne (Nashville)
Sawyer, John (Cape Coral, Florida)
Shelton, Aaron (New Johnsonville, Tennessee)
Simpkins, Ozell (Nashville)
Smith, Christine Johnson (Owensboro, Kentucky)
Smith, Fleming (Nashville)
Summers, Walt (Nashville)
Unruh, Von (Kingston Springs, Tennessee)
Waugh,Irving (Nashville)
White, Ellery Wagner (Nashville)
Wallace, Wilbert (Nashville)
Williams, Michael E. (Nashville)
Wills, W. Ridley, II (Franklin, Tennessee)
Young, H. Calvin, Jr. (Nashville)

Journals and Periodicals
Arendale, Marirose. "Tennessee and Woman's Rights." *Tennessee Historical Quarterly* 34 (spring 1980): 62–78.
Billboard, 7, 30 August 1947; 27 December 1947; 3, 24 January 1948.
Broadcasting, 28 January 1963.
Coleman, Emily. "Disk from Dixie." *Newsweek*, 15 September 1947.
Craig, C. A. "Craig Tops Hit Parade with 'Near You.'" *Scroll of Phi Delta Theta* (January 1948).
Dalton, Martin L. "Blalock and Harrison—A Rare Friendship." *Pharos of Alpha Omega Alpha*, 61 (summer 1998): 26–31.
DeWitt, John H., Jr. "Early Radio Broadcasting in Middle Tennessee."

Tennessee Historical Quarterly 31 (spring 1972): 80–94.
Falzarano, Gino. "The Kitty Kallen Story." Sony Music Entertainment, 1992.
Flans, Robyn. "The History of Nashville Recording." *Mix*, March 1998, 66.
Grantham, Dewey W. "Tennessee and Twentieth-Century Politics." *Tennessee Historical Quarterly* 54 (fall 1995): 214.
Hay, George. "History of WSM from the Memorable Inaugural Program October 5th, 1925." *Broadcast News of the Week*, 12 November 1932.
Keel, Beverly. "Mr. Guitar." *Nashville Life* (December, January 1998).
Langhammer, Jay. "Phis in Arts and Entertainment." *Scroll of Phi Delta Theta* (spring 1997).
"Nashville Historical Commission Marks First Radio Station Site at Belmont University." *Circle* 36 (fall/winter 1997–98): 1.
Nashville This Week, 24–31 January 1927; 2–9 April 1928; 16–23 September 1929; 3–10 March 1930.
Ragland Reporter, October 1947.
Rumble, John. "The Emergence of Nashville as a Recording Center, Logbooks from the Castle Studio, 1952–1953." *Journal of Country Music* (December 1978): 22–41
"The Story Behind the Song." *Juke Box Comics*. New York: Famous Funnies, Inc. September 1948.
Time Magazine, 12 January 1948.
Variety, 17 September 1947–10 January 1948.
Wills, Ridley II. "The Old Boys' Schools of Middle Tennessee." *Tennessee Historical Quarterly* (spring 1997): 56, 67

Newspapers
Asheville Citizen Times
Birmingham Age-Herald
Birmingham News-Age Herald
Central Florida Ocala Times
Cherry Point Wind Sock
Colorado City Post Telegram
Denver Rocky Mountain News
Dickson Free Press
Dickson Home Enterprise
Nashville American
Nashville Banner
Nashville Magazine
Nashville Scene
Nashville Tennessean

In 1972, the name of this newspaper was changed to *The Tennessean*. To maintain consistency, I have used *NT* throughout for abbreviation.

Nashville Tennessean Magazine
New York Enquirer
New York Times
New York Times Biographical Service
Our Shield
Pittsburgh Post-Gazette
Ragland Reporter
Shield News
Toledo Sunday Times
University of Alabama Crimson-White
Unknown Pulaski, Tennessee newspaper
Vanderbilt Hustler
Wall Street Journal
Westview

Collections, Papers, and Other Sources
Bullet Recording Co. catalog. Country Foundation and Media Center, Nashville.
Cigar Classics, Volume One, The Standards. Universal City, Calif.: Universal Music Special Markets, Inc., 1997. Compact disc.
Country Music Hall of Fame archives, Nashville.
Francis Craig Papers. Special Collections Section. Jean and Alexander Heard Library, Vanderbilt University, Nashville.
Francis Craig. Vanderbilt University transcript. Joan and Alexander Heard Library, Vanderbilt University, Nashville.
DesPrez, Roger M. "Tuberculosis Treatment—Old and New." Medicine Grand Rounds. Vanderbilt University School of Medicine. Videocassette #M-1519, 25 May 1995.
Grubin, David, and Judy Crichton. *America 1900*. Corporation for Public Broadcasting, 1998.
Ingram, Bowen. "The Story of Francis Craig." MSS. Lebanon, Tennessee, c. 1950.
Irene Beasley Papers. University of Maryland Libraries, College Park, Maryland.
"Nostalgia News Report." *Pages of Time 1938*. Millersville: Tenn.: n.p.
Rumble, John. "Fred Rose and the Development of the Nashville Music

Industry." Ph.D. diss., Vanderbilt University, 1980.
Shelton, Aaron."The Story of Castle Recording Lab." In *Autobiography*. N.p., 1990 [?].
Showler, Joe. "Time for T." Vernon Films. MCS Recording Studio, Toronto.
WSM Radio & TV file. Special Collections Section. Jean and Alexander Heard Library, Vanderbilt University Library, Nashville.

Government and Institutional Publications
Will Beasley, *Nashville Music City USA*. Nashville's Partnership 2000. Nashville: Nashville Chamber of Commerce, n.d.
Billboard 1995 Music Yearbook. Menomenee Falls, Wis.: Record Research, Inc., 1996.
Fifteenth Census of the United States, 1930. Vol. 3, pt 2. Washington: United States Census Office, 1932.
Historical Statistics of the United States: Colonial Times to 1970. Washington, D.C.: United States Department of Commerce, 1975.
Marshall-Bruce-Polk Cos.'s Nashville City Directory 1926. Nashville: Marshall-Bruce-Polk.
MCA Records, Inc. Historical Catalogue. Vol. 2. Universal City, Calif., 31 December 1979.
Metropolitan Nashville Register of Deeds. 20737. Bk. 716.
Pen and Sunlight Sketches of Nashville. Reprint. Hermitage Hotel folder in Nashville Room, Nashville Public Library.
"Statistical Record of Nashville 1966–1967." Nashville Area Chamber of Commerce.
Twelfth Census of the United States, 1900. Vol. 1. Washington: United States Census Office, 1901.
Vanderbilt Alumni Directory. Vol. 1. Nashville: Vanderbilt University Alumni Association, 1923
Vanderbilt Alumnus, December 1942; September–October 1961; spring 1982.
Vanderbilt Commodore, 1919; 1922; 1930.
Vanderbilt University catalog, 1918–1920.

About the Compact Disc

The compact disc presents a sound perspective of Francis Craig's career—his style of music, his thoughts, his big hit, "Near You." It is derived mainly from tapes of radio broadcasts, many on WSM-AM. The Berryhill interview tapes on tracks 2 and 15 are courtesy of the Mary and Ken Berryhill Collection. The compact disc was mastered by Jerry Gowen of Jerry Gowen Digital. The sound of Craig's orchestras and his melodious southern voice help to convey the essence of the man and his music.

1. **"Red Rose."** Craig reminisces about his theme song on a Hollywood interview program, *Meet the Music Makers*, c. spring 1948. The rendition, smoothy introduced by Jud Collins, was on a "Francis Craig Serenade" show—vocal by Bob Lamm.

2. **The Jazz Age—"That Florida Low-Down," "Steady Roll Blues," and "Hard-to-Get Gertie."**—These three songs were recorded in Atlanta in the early years of Craig's band (see discography). Craig's comments before "That Florida Low-Down" were to an unknown WSM announcer on a late 1930s show called *Personality of the Day*. Remarks after the same song, again discussing Jimmy Melton, were to Ken Berryhill, who was interviewing Francis for Berryhill's and Tom Landess's "Old Record Shop" program at Vanderbilt on station WMAK, 24 January 1952.

3. **His Kind of Music—"Sometimes I Wonder."** In the 1930s interview noted above, Francis verbalizes his preference for dreamy music. "Sometimes I Wonder," another Bob Lamm vocal, is from another "Francis Craig Serenade." Francis cowrote this song (see catalogue).

4. **Francis Craig and Snooky Lanson—"Body and Soul."** Bob Stitch of station WAMB interviews Snooky Lanson on their last program together, 23 May 1987. They play Snooky's version of "Body and Soul,"

from an early forties Craig orchestra WSM broadcast.

5. **Francis Craig and Kitty Kallen—"I Love You Too Much."** Jo Sherman of WSM interviews Francis in 1962. The ballad was sung by Kitty on WSM sometime in early 1940.

6. **"Dynamite."** From the same Sherman interview, Francis conveys how excited he was to write Vanderbilt's official fight song. The first version of "Dynamite" is by the Vanderbilt glee club, the second, probably in the early forties, by the studio orchestra. Ernie Keller is the announcer.

7. **"Tennessee Tango."** This is one of several songs written by Francis and Beasley Smith after "Near You" (see catalogue). The arrangements were duplicative, and all the vocals were by Bob Lamm. None was a hit.

8. **"Disallusioned."** It is unknown why this title was spelled this way.

9. **"Hot Biscuits."** Francis loved songs with southern themes.

10. **Francis Craig and Red Foley—"Alabama Jubilee."** This recording from the Jo Sherman interview demonstrates Red Foley's wonderful voice and a lighter side of Francis Craig.

11. **"The *Nashville Banner* March."** After Craig's peppy piano solo, we hear a truly grand rendering by Don Estes backed by the Anita Kerr Singers.

12. **"Beg Your Pardon."** From the Hollywood "Meet the Music Makers" interview, Francis explains

the rationale for his second big hit. His classical training comes through in the flowery introductory arpeggio.

13. **The Original "Near You."** In his own words, Francis explains on ". . . Music Makers" to "Ira," the announcer, why he wrote the song and how it took off. The first few bars are from a tape of the original recording and are very scratchy. The clear portion was pulled from the Jo Sherman interview show. Note the ending words by Bob Lamm. Afterwards, Francis explains to Jo Sherman when and why the ending was changed.

14. **Comedic "Near You."** Ernie Keller introduces a show of unknown date. Apparently from the Ryman Auditorium, it was to celebrate the unbelievable success of Craig's song. The deep, talented WSM staff renders successively operatic, Hawaiian, and country versions of Craig's pop hit. They were clever. From Spike Jones's "Spotlight Revue" network program of 14 November 1947, we hear a mangled "Near You." The announcer is Mike Wallace. No song is sacred to Spike.

15. **A Lush "Near You."** Francis discusses with Ken Berryhill in 1952 just how big "Near You" was vis-à-vis the previous champ, "My Blue Heaven." "Near You" could be rendered in many ways. Note the changed ending words from this c. 1948 NBC show.

16. **"Goodnight, Sweetheart."** From the 1 January 1947 "Francis Craig Serenade," a velvet-voiced Irving Waugh bids adieu. This was nineteen days before "Near You" was recorded and some six months before Craig disbanded his orchestra.

—— *Music Publication Information* ——

Alabama Jubilee: Jerome H. Remick. Composers Jack Yellen and George L. Cobb.

Beg Your Pardon: Robbins Music Corp., 1947. Bullet 1012, date unknown.

Body and Soul: Warner Brothers, Inc./Chappel and Company, Ltd. Words by Edward Hayman, Robert Sour, and Frank Eyton, music by John Green.

Disallusioned: Bullet 1040, date unknown.

Dynamite (When Vandy Starts to Fight): Edwin H. Morris & Co., Inc.

Goodnight, Sweetheart: Campbell-Connelly Co., Ltd./Robins Music Corp. Composers Ray Noble, James Campbell, Reg Connelly.

Hard-to-Get Gertie: Columbia 709-D, 1926.

Hot Biscuits: Arrow Music Co., n.d.

I Love You Too Much: MCA Music. Writers Don Raye and Alex Olshanetski.

The *Nashville Banner* March: *Nashville Banner* Publishing Co., 1951.

Near You: Supreme Music Corp., 1947. Bullet 1001, 1947. Decca 28089, 1952. MCA p-2710, 1980.

Red Rose: Forster Music Publisher, Inc., 1937. Columbia 1544-D, 1928. Bullet 1001, 1947.

Steady Roll Blues: Columbia 567-D, 1925.

Sometimes I Wonder: Edwin H. Morris & Co., Inc., 1945.

Tennessee Tango: Robbins Music Corp., n.d. MGM 10378, 1949.

That Florida Low-Down: Columbia 1266-D, 1926.

Index

NEAR YOU

Lyric by
KERMIT GOELL

Music by
FRANCIS CRAIG